THE INSIDER'S
GUIDE
TO PARIS

THE INSIDER'S GUIDE TO PARIS

KATE MUIR

ROBSON BOOKS

First published in Great Britain in 1999 by Robson Books,
10 Blenheim Court, Brewery Road, London N7 9NT

British Library Cataloguing in Publication Data
A catalogue record for this title is available from the British Library

ISBN 1 86105 165 4

Designed by Peter Ward.
Set in 13 on 14pt Perpetua with Trajan display type.

Printed in Great Britain by
WBC Book Manufacturers, Bridgend, Mid Glamorgan

CONTENTS

LOVERS' PARIS

CULTURAL PARIS

PARIS AFTER DARK

CHILDREN'S PARIS

ACKNOWLEDGEMENTS

I would like to thank everyone at *The Times*, particularly my editors Gill Morgan and Brian McArthur for their help with this book. Liane Katz was a superb researcher and rollerblader. Thanks also to Kate Mills at Robson Books, and to my agent Gill Coleridge.

INTRODUCTION

This is not your normal guide to Paris, for the city of light and the city of dreams has also become the city of the swift Awayday Return from Britain. This is a book for people who know too much — for those who want to make the upgrade from tourist to native, if only for the weekend.

Nowadays, Paris is the light at the end of the tunnel, a train journey away and a culture apart. What could be better? I live here at the end of the Eurostar line, on the Left Bank of the Seine. I've done so for three years, while producing a weekly column for *The Times* and two children. Of course, when you move somewhere as enduringly pleasant and convenient as Paris, you get a lot of weekend guests. So many that we renamed their resting place the Eurostar Memorial Sofabed (EMS).

This guide was born from the demands of EMS users in the Rue du Bac. We don't touch on the mainstream stuff like the Eiffel Tower, the Musée d'Orsay or the Galeries Lafayette. No, your typical sofabed-users want to impress friends back home by attending a Sunday-morning debate at a philosophers' café. They want to know the most marvellous little back-street bistro which does rabbit stuffed with mint and *chèvre* and is run by a poet; the address of the best taxidermist in Paris; and the site of a small but perfectly formed town-house museum – the Jacquemart-André – which has the finest Uccellos around and serves delicious pastries in the dining-room.

This is by no means a comprehensive guide to the city, and intended to be that way – you can consult the Michelin or Fodor for directions to Disneyland Paris. Instead, this prides itself on being as idiosyncratic and biased as possible. Let's face it: you're not a part of the polyester-clad coach parties in front of the Mona Lisa, and neither am I. Instead, I hand my bizarre explorations to you on a plate, topped with a survivor's guide for those who wish to avoid committing the sort of social and gastro-nomic *faux pas* which invite sneers from true Parisians.

I love it here, and I hope that comes across. I knew it, really, the day we first arrived from the train at the Gare du Nord. We were at the back of the taxi queue with four suitcases and a very tired baby. Suddenly, the queue parted like the Red Sea, and battalions of French ladies ushered us to the front saying, '*Bébé, bébé.*' The only grumblers as we passed were tourists.

GASTRONOMIC
PARIS

CHEESE SHOPS

Primed to explode at 8.30pm

'The Camembert with its gamey scent of venison had conquered the more muffled tones of Maroilles and Limbourg . . . Into the middle of this vigorous phrase the Parmesan threw its thin note on a country flute, while the Brie added the dull gentleness of damp tambourines.'

Thus wrote Emile Zola on the Paris cheese shop, and little has changed today. My local cheese shop, Barthélémy[1], turns out to be one of the greatest in Paris – small but wildly ambitious. The soft cheeses are so ripe they almost pass out on the plate, and the hard are dignified with age.

The shop on Rue de Grenelle has old tiled floors sprinkled daily with sawdust and marble counters covered with straw matting from which the cheese rises in piles: wobbling Reblochons; Brébis – sheeps' cheese – from Corsica; fishy-smelling Tomme; heart-shaped Coeur de Neufchâtel; ancient, cracked Mimoulette and spoonable Mont d'Or, as well as 40 different goats' cheeses. On Saturdays, a queue stretches outside the door, the 240 varieties leaving little room for customers.

Even when closed on Sundays and Mondays, the scent of cheese mutating in the cellars percolates into the street, and there are those who swear that the money from the cashpoint at the bank next door smells of fine Roquefort.

Roland Barthélémy, the *maître fromager*, is a splendid figure in a sort of medical coat embroidered with his name. We quit the pungent shop for a corner café to discuss his art.

Make no mistake, it is an art. Monsieur Barthélémy travels 5,000 kilometres a year visiting his suppliers in the countryside. He squeezes, tastes and sniffs out the finest cheeses in their cellars, and marks them as his own, leaving them to age to perfection before delivery to his shops in Paris and Fontainebleau.

In 25 years, he has become a couturier of cheese, while others are merely *prêt-à-porter*. Other *fromagers* may supply bistro chains, but M. Barthélémy caters for the finest dinner parties on the Left Bank, as well as President Chirac, Prime Minister Lionel Jospin at his nearby residence, Matignon, and most of the foreign embassies.

'I care about giving the pleasure of taste more than just running a business,' says M. Barthélémy over espresso. He takes off his glasses and closes his eyes as the words pour out. 'I have to visit the cheeses myself where they are made – it's the nose, the human contact, the need to see that the conditions are just right.'

In the cellar under the shop, he allows the soft cheeses to ripen for between one and three weeks. 'There are three essentials for *l'affinage* [the ripening process]: temperature, kept at 8°C, humidity, and ventilation which allows the mould to grow in the cheese.'

The word 'pasteurised' is not in M. Barthélémy's

vocabulary. Pasteurised milk means dead, bland cheese, and he prefers raw milk cheeses which have a life of their own.

His staff of matronly ladies in white coats and matching wellingtons always know just which cheese is at its peak that day, or indeed that hour. On my virginal visit to the shop, I innocently said: 'Half a Camembert, please.' The matrons looked aghast, appalled not only that I wanted a half, but that I had neither specified a particular Camembert, nor informed them of the time of consumption. 'Is it for lunch, this evening or tomorrow?' asked one lady. 'Tonight,' I said, and she presented me with a cheese primed, like a gooey bomb, to go off at precisely 8.30pm.

Now if, say, Jacques Chirac or myself were having a dinner party for ten and wanted a cheeseboard, what would M. Barthélémy recommend for July, each cheese having its season? 'Well, I would give you six cheeses perfect for tonight, a little of each, so nothing is left over. I would start with a Camembert, a Roquefort at its peak, an old Gruyère de Fribourg, a half Reblochon, and two little goats' cheeses, one ripe and tender, and one dry.'

For travellers, M. Barthélémy can provide the same cheeseboard, in a special sealed bag 'so as not to upset your neighbours on the Eurostar', but the cheeses will be slightly less ripe so they last the journey, peaking on English soil. I once was going on holiday to Italy, and I asked him to put together a cheeseboard that would be perfect in three days' time, allowing for plane and taxi travel, as well as fridge storage. It was, and I do not exaggerate, a poem.

There are many other fine cheese shops, each with their own idiosyncracies and specialities, such as Alléosse[2], La Ferme St Hubert[3], and for one-stop supermarket gastronomy, the Grande Epicerie of the Bon Marché[4]. One should never underestimate the importance of serving perhaps just one, perfect cheese, especially when guests are French. As the first foodie, Anthelme Brillat-Savarin noted in the politically incorrect days of 1825: 'Dessert without cheese is like a pretty girl with only one eye.'

1 BARTHELEMY, 51 Rue de Grenelle, 7th, M Rue du Bac,
     01 45 48 56 75.
2 ALLEOSSE, 13 Rue Poncelet, 17th, M Ternes, 46 22 50 45.
3 LA FERME ST HUBERT, 21 Rue Vignon, 8th, M Madeleine,
     47 42 79 20.
4 LE BON MARCHE GRANDE EPICERIE, 38 Rue de Sèvres,
     M Sèvres-Babylone, 01 44 39 80 00.
For cheese shop list: *The Food Lover's Guide to Paris*, by Patricia Wells, Workman Publishing.

❝Have been making detailed observations of the daily deliveries to the government ministries along the 63 bus route on the Quai d'Orsay. My attention was first drawn by a van from the best cheese shop in Paris outside the Ministry of the Army. Then I noticed the finest *pâtissier* was making regular visits to the Ministry of Urbanism and Housing. Passing the police headquarters, we had a close shave with a van belonging to a wine merchant of the highest repute. Beer and sandwiches are clearly out of the question for French ministers visiting Britain.

❝Despite the fact that we live in the country with the finest bread in the world, I often find myself pathetically sneaking a multigrain Harry's American Sandwich Loaf into my trolley in the Bon Marché. The fault of the French baguette lies in its very freshness, its lack of preservatives, which renders it inedible hours after purchase and minutes after slicing. For those of us too untogether to put on full make-up, earrings and high heels to walk over to the *boulangerie* before breakfast every morning, Harry's loaf is a godsend.

Paris mamans, it emerges, rely on Pain de Poilâne, the designer handmade sourdough bread from Rue du Cherche-Midi, which lasts a day or two. The Space-Hopper-sized Poilâne loaves are sold in bags depicting great moments in the history of bread, including the birth of Britain's John Montagu de Sandwich in 1718.

Puzzlingly, there are two opposing patron saints of *boulangers*: the poverty-stricken St Roch (1295–1327) who was famously kept alive by a dog that brought him bread every day, and the snootier St Honoré (600), the bishop of Amiens, who is suspected of having a personal baker, the Dark Ages equivalent of a personal trainer.

For a long time, I assumed other families tossed away their stumps of yesterday's baguette, until a native of Toulouse showed me the artisanal 'refreshing' technique. You stick the loaf in the microwave for 30 seconds and it becomes deliciously soft. Of course, it reverts straight back to rock inside your stomach. Inspired, the husband now favours microwaving yesterday's croissants with Marmite and butter inside, which turn to warm Play-Doh.

Our *boulanger* on the Rue de Grenelle makes initially delicious baguettes which develop a granite-like resistance to a knife in around five hours. It reminds me of that Roald Dahl short story where a wife kills her errant husband with the frozen Sunday joint, then cooks the blunt instrument and serves it to the investigating policemen. Our day-old baguette is equally promising.

SUNDAY FOOD MARKETS

Sandalled eco-Parisians

On Sundays, Paris can be strangely dead. French families disappear indoors to create the perfect *grande bouffe* lunch – not forgetting cheeses and *tarte tatin* (caramelized apple tart) – creating wafts of exquisite daubes from the big double doors that slam on the secret courtyards of Haussmannian apartments. The families only re-emerge towards 4pm, bloated and well oiled, either to take children to the park or to visit the *patisserie* to select a *gâteau* for afternoon tea at the grandparents'.

The tourist observing this closet gastronomy is naturally jealous, if not tearful, and a bistro lunch only goes some way to ameliorate the pain. The solution is to do as the French do on such mornings – head to the outdoor food markets for a feast to take home, either for a picnic on the train or an impressive dinner in Britain the day after.

A Sunday tour of my local markets on the Left Bank started with the famed Rue de Buci and Rue de Seine' just off Boulevard St Germain. This market is picturesque, but by no means the cheapest – it is said that many of the stalls are owned by one businessman. However, the produce is superb. The cheese stalls were a hedonist's delight – we did not buy sensibly for the week, but for the moment – squeezing soft Reblochons and Pont l'Eveques bulging at the sides with ripeness.

In Rue de Seine is Le Fournil de Pierre bakery (a good chain) with its slogan 'Pierre takes his own hands to the dough'. The result is delicious crusty homemade bread, mini-rectangular wholegrain loaves and a squint country baguette to take home. The markets are also friendly, traffic-free places for small children, with glorious sights and smells all at pram level, never mind little tastings offered by sympathetic stallholders. Adult tastings are even better. If it was cold and crisp we were offered sips of hefty winter reds at the wine stall, accompanied by a morsel of cheese – pleasant just after breakfast. The customers here were nearly all French and very picky – this would be a fine place to find a few bargains to take home.

While we were at the mushroom stall selecting pleurotes and girolles over trompettes and cèpes, all at affordable prices, a courageous woman in a fur coat bought morilles at Fr299 a kilo.

For those who fear home cooking, this market is also surrounded by *traiteurs* – delicatessens selling perfect ready-made meals – whose existence allows the Paris madame to avoid the heat of the kitchen and remain *soignée*. There are homemade pastas, stuffed peppers and colourful slices of terrine, pleasingly composed of lentils layered with *foie gras*, wild mushrooms, or baby vegetables.

Across the road is the Marché St Germain², which used to be a proper covered market. Now, however, it has been modernized and filled by shops like Monsoon and

Gap, as well as an Irish bar. The remaining foodhall is small, although useful on a rainy day.

There are Buci-style markets throughout Paris all week except Mondays. The remains of the old Les Halles market is in Rue Montorgueil[3], where many Paris chefs shop in the mornings. A coffee break should be taken at number 51 for the Stohrer pastries. In the Latin Quarter, the narrow Rue Mouffetard[4] is picturesque, filled with old shop signs, some restored Louis XIII fronts, and – unfortunately – a few too many tourists.

A Sunday-only event – and in my opinion, the best of the lot – is the morning 'bio' farmers' market on the Boulevard Raspail[5]. As we approached down Rue Cherche-Midi, we smelt the cheese and onion galettes in the wind. We bought a few organic courgettes and ugly-looking tomatoes, which somehow produced a ratatouille that tasted rather than merely looked good, accompanied by homemade farm sausages. There were also odd-shaped squashes and pumpkins, unavailable anywhere else. The homemade multigrain or herb bread is a delightful escape from the tedious baguette.

This market is best for people-spotting, for French film stars, and because it's the only place where hairy Parisians can be spotted wearing trek sandals and socks, shopping at stalls selling unbleached linen and cotton undershirts and baby rompers. The farmers drive in from the country bearing bunches of autumn leaves and berries – far better than hothouse flowers – along with their unpasteurised cheeses and yoghurts, chestnut honey, apple cider and (formerly) happy hens.

66 The relationship with one's local commerçants is all-
important here: after a while, the butcher will hold a
hot roast chicken for you until evening, the deli will
cut your salami just so, and the vegetable shop will
throw free herbs into your bag.

My French girlfriend who lives in the 15th
arrondissement had formed a marvellous friendship with
her greengrocer – her toddler was allowed to run
behind the counter, the child's mouth was stuffed with
cherries and the baby was declared beautiful at least
twice a week. But one day Mme Légume, as we shall
call her, suggested that perhaps the baby was not
dressed warmly enough and seemed sick. My friend –
who had had a stressful day – retorted that her child
was warm, in perfect health and merely dribbling.

There was a stony silence, which lasted for weeks,
and then months. Mme Légume took her money, but
refused to meet her eye or explain. Desperate – for
the veg was very good – my friend wrote a letter
apologizing for any unintended insult. An equally

formal reply came from Mme Légume, acknowledging that my friend had been rude, not merely in refusing advice on her children's health but by bringing bags containing *(quelle horreur)* supermarket apples into the shop. Despite this, Madame magnanimously offered to forgive, forget and furnish future vegetables.

"Been a bosky week or two here, so I have suspended my no-cooking rule to embrace girolles, chanterelles, ceps and trompettes de mort sautéed in a little butter and olive oil – it is wild mushroom season and it would be churlish not to join the national pig-in. I like finding a free-range pine needle or blade of grass in my fricassée at Sunday lunch and wondering whether we will we live to see the coffee or die writhing from the joker poisonous toadstool in the pack. Although the black trompettes de mort are all verbal front and no action, the ceps oozing greeny-yellow fur on their undersides are much scarier, yet turn creamy in the pan. After lunch, it's nice to remind diners of the plot in John Lanchester's *The Debt to Pleasure* which centres on a murder by killer mushroom, exquisitely cooked. Wild mushroom picking *en famille* is *the* quintessentially French activity, since it is a) multi-generational; b) it occurs in the great French *campagne*; and c) there's a slap-up scoff afterwards. It has become a signpost in literature and films to show family bonding. Sighing 'I remember when we used to go mushrooming together in the autumn woods' is the Gallic equivalent of that moment in American films when characters reach intimacy by sharing a significant event in their childhood. 'I remember when Pop first took me to the ball

game/trout fishing/the jail to see Mom' etc. That
magic mushroom moment is more poignant for some,
however, since around 300 amateur pickers pass away
every year when they mis-identify toadstools.

HÉDIARD
AND
FAUCHON

Madeleine bun fight

The opposing armies face one another across the Place de la Madeleine, waiting each morning for battle to commence. In the right-hand corner, uniformed in brown, is Fauchon[1], and in the left, wearing red, Hédiard[2].

Paris's grandest food emporia – sworn enemies – watch each other's every move. Their weaponry is displayed in terrifying price tags and competing window displays, oozing with crystallized fruit, slabs of chocolate and pungent game birds.

Fortunately for any serious foodie, or even foodievoyeur, there are reasons to go to both shops, for each has its strengths. Fauchon is the more exhaustive, with 20,000 products, enormous fresh food counters and a daily *patisserie* display to die for.

Hédiard has a smaller range of 6,000 products, but is in some ways *plus snob*, as the Parisians say, with its exquisite red and black packaging and powerful smell of coffee.

Auguste Fauchon's empire started as an exotic fruit stall on the Madeleine 110 years ago and has expanded to cover half a block, including five restaurants. Ferdinand Hédiard had a head start, however, opening his first spice and fruit shop in Paris in 1850 and moving to the Madeleine in 1854.

M. Fauchon claims to have brought the first avocados to the city and was forced to give them away to doubting customers. However, M. Hédiard was first with the pineapple, tested on his friends Eugène Delacroix and Alexandre Dumas.

Thus the noble lineage of neither shop is in doubt. Fauchon is rather old-fashioned, but behind every counter is an expert who will go into extreme detail if encouraged. A *sommelier* will take you on a tour of the stone wine cellar, stretching in a warren under the streets, pointing out Taittinger champagne in bottles, designed by Roy Lichtenstein, and an affordable little Pouilly Fuissé at Fr44.

In the *patisserie* window at present there are slices of foot-tall cake, topped by an enormous cherry, each slice being a cake in itself, sealed in chocolate. The tourists are forced to buy less fragile items, so the English buy mustard and the Japanese buy tea, both easily obtained on native soil. Then there are Fr15 jams, including rose petal and jasmine.

Hédiard also does extraordinary jams and jellies in small, homemade-style batches, including a curious marmalade with entire slices of orange packing the jar. The coffee counter will grind beans and brew a test cup of your chosen blend, and there are teas by the dozen, some set out for tasting beneath signs saying 'The 1999 First-Flush Darjeeling has arrived!'

The shop has modernized however, and there are four Hédiards in Paris and distributors throughout the world. Its first-floor restaurant was refurbished recently in cherrywood and colonial-style chairs covered in fake leopard and zebra skin, making a chic, but not cheap, place for lunch.

Hédiard's specialities, baskets of exotic fruits, chocolates and even mini-vegetables – artichokes like small roses with tiny carrots for foliage – can be home-delivered by a bellhop in uniform wearing a hat saying 'Groom Etoile'. Both Fauchon and Hédiard have discovered a growing market in prepared dinners, duck or fish in complex sauces that allow the Parisian working woman to give a dinner party without entering the kitchen.

This is food that transcends mere cookery. On Hédiard's wall, a notice says: 'Conviviality is the dish of the day, laughter is drunk like a good wine, ideas are good like good bread, exquisite flavours of sweet desserts make your company even more beautiful and good coffee gives wings.'

1 FAUCHON, 26, Place de la Madeleine, M Madeleine, 8th, 01 47 42 60 11.
2 HÉDIARD, 21, Place de la Madeleine, 8th, M Madeleine, 01 43 12 88 88.
3 LA GRANDE EPICERIE, BON MARCHE, (stocks Fauchon goods and other specialities) 38 Rue de Sèvres, 7th, M Sèvres-Babylone, 01 44 39 81 00.

❝Have just learnt a new word: gastrophilosophe. This is fortunate, for a British friend who can only be described as a great culinary thinker was over on the Eurostar Memorial Sofabed last weekend, and I was able to apply the term. This particular gastrophilosophe believes that the essence of every French restaurant is

to be found in its *crème brûlée*. If the dessert is eggy
and soggy, the top not sufficiently caramelized and
crunchy – then the entire establishment fails in his
book. Fortunately, during the gastrophilosophe's
Stakhanovite stay – eating a *brûlée* with every meal is
no picnic – he lighted upon a version in a wide dish
with more surface area, which improved the ratio of
crisp top to cream. It was flavoured with lime and
basil, and on tasting he pronounced it 'daring but
exceptional'. We all breathed a sigh of relief.

Gastrophilosophes are not merely interested in the
inner man but the inner animal, and eat a great deal of
offal and other scary cuts. Sadly, our own gastrophilosophe ordered a pig's trotter in breadcrumbs
at a somewhat ordinary bistro. He was expecting it
stuffed, maybe marinated. But when it arrived, it was
a sad little stumpy leg, still bearing the occasional hair.
Bravely our friend tackled the sinewy limb, and then
backed off. 'There's something about toenails on a
plate . . .' he said.

TAKING TEA

Analysis of divine pastries

The Paris foot soldier needs serious fuel, so it's imperative to have a good *salon de thé* mapped into your route. Once oddities, teashops are now available in every *arrondissement*, from the traditional ones started last century, to the newest and hippest in the Marais.

If you like strong coffee and lighting, coupled with PVC banquettes, café life is fine. By the afternoon, however, in the average corner café, the croissants are slightly stale. The apple tart has been solidifying in the fridge all day, and the tea is often a dusty bag resting beside a glass of warm water. If, after a long cold walk, you wish to sink into a squashy armchair and a perfect *tarte tatin*, then the tearoom is the only sensible solution.

My favourite of the grand old teashops is Ladurée[1] by the Madeleine, also convenient for ladies who dedicate their lives to shopping in the Rue du Faubourg St Honoré. The green and gold canopied shop opened in 1862, and inside it looks as if it has not been painted since – the ceilings abound with badly executed cupids, and the walls are mirrored and gilded to the nines. The clientele is gilded too – no earring is too small here, no bag clasp too shiny, no shoe is without its Gucci snaffle. Ladies of a certain age lunch here and scoff enormous pastries without a gold button popping.

The waitresses are properly dressed with frilly pinnies, and the service is friendly, since ladies often have to change tables to cement certain social connections. Outside, a crowd usually surrounds the windows taking in what can only be described as a pornographic display. There is a full-size chocolate bust of Marie Antoinette with meringues and roses for hair and a bustier of macaroons. Nearby are mini-pastries, éclairs, tiny and giant tarts bursting with glazed fruit. One mini-tart has three perfect raspberries suspended in cream on a pastry disc. It is divine.

Ladurée is not cheap. That is the point. Tea at a marbled-topped table varies between Fr31 and Fr35, depending on which exquisite variety you order, and comes with leaves in the silver pot and a matching silver hot water jug. A croissant is Fr7, pastries around Fr20, but worth every bite. For a light lunch, the Fr51 *tarte aux poireaux* (leeks) with a bowl of green salad is much favoured. The pastry flakes away and melts, the egg barely restrains chunks of buttery leek.

Recently, Ladurée – plush and flush with success – opened a mega-tea-room on the Champs-Elysées.[2] The food's the same, but the decor has more icing. Napoleon III would have been proud of the magnificent marbles, the smiling caryatids, and the Romanesque murals.

The French favour Ladurée, while the tourists are sent to the more expensive Angelina.[3] This is Paris's most famous tea-room, with Versailles-style mirrors and murals, and is much more spacious than the fuggy Ladurée. For

Fr36, Angelina does do the best hot chocolate in Paris, involving melted chocolate bars and whipped cream in bowls. A glass of water is supplied to calm the customer. However, commercialized souvenirs and the clientele makes the place look like Tokyo or New York. The English translation of the menu – 'egg custard toast with bacon strips' – is enough to put you off your quiche Lorraine.

Down in the Marais, there has been an outbreak of newer teashops, satisfying in a different way. The most comforting, and comfortable, is Les Enfants Gâtés[4] on the Rue Francs-Bourgeois, which Marais-goers know to be shopping central. There are old leather armchairs, wicker Lloyd Looms, yellowed walls and slices of *tarte tatin* at Fr40 which could easily serve an entire family. Warm, the apples repose stickily by a pile of crème fraîche.

Les Enfants Gâtés also does, from 11am, one of the best brunches in the city, which comes in sizes small, medium, large and extra large.

For those who wish to dine outdoors, or take some *mille-feuille* home to the land of dull crumpets, there are fabulous individual corner *patisseries*, which may be assessed by the beauty and expense of their windows. One particularly good shop is Christian Constant[5] and the city-wide chain Dalloyau[6], which open on Sunday afternoons so that the mother-in-law (ironically *la belle-mère*) may be placated with a gift of pink and pistaccio-coloured macaroons, or a perfect chocolate cake.

1   LADUREE, 16 Rue Royale, 8th, M Madeleine, 01 42 60 21 79.

2   LADUREE, 75 Avenue des Champs-Elysées, 8th, M George V,
      01 40 75 08 75.

3   ANGELINA, 226 Rue de Rivoli, 1st, M Tuileries, 01 42 60 82 00.

4   LES ENFANTS GATE, 43 Rue des Francs-Bourgeois, 4th, M St

"Many here have been saddened by the news that French blood-donor centres will no longer be offering a restorative pint of red wine to those who have just drained away. 'We will, however, be serving non-alcoholic cider,' reveals the Parisian centre.

Still, the gastronomic benefits of becoming a blood donor here remain enticing. 'Depending on the time of day, we offer various meals and snacks,' they say. A particularly popular lunch for donors is the selection of hams and salamis, followed by *poulet basquais* or paella, finishing with *tarte aux fraises* or a simple fruit compôte. The breakfast pastries are said to be particularly buttery, and hot chocolate is offered, along with coffee.

'It's a far cry from the tea and custard-cream you get in Glasgow,' I said to a French friend. 'Last time I gave blood there I fainted in a tunnel by Cowcaddens Underground station and everyone left me well alone with the sticking plaster on my arm, thinking I was a junkie.'

Yes, she agreed, she'd fainted too the only time she gave blood. Indeed she was worried that blood-donor centres offered hot chocolate to the newly sapped. 'You see, I also fainted after the hot chocolate at Angelinas.' Naturally, some are unable to steel themselves against this divine sugar rush, and it was

thus that my French friend found herself flat on her
back outside the Angelina tea-room on the Rue de
Rivoli, being revived by a handsome man who was
holding her legs in the air and making the questionable
statement: 'Mademoiselle, I'm a doctor.'

" To dunk or not to dunk – that is the question
worrying Le Tout Paris. The debate began when a
respected gastrophilosophe, Jean-Paul Gené,
suggested: 'It is time that the art of dunking should be
outed from the shadows where it has been relegated
by outdated table manners.' Gené, acknowledged
leader of the Nouveaux Trempeurs, or New Dunkers
movement, has chronicled the sufferings and
deprivations caused by useless etiquette.

The French would never be so vulgar as to open a
restaurant chain unashamedly called 'Dunkin' Donuts',
but the unspoken urge is equally strong. In the Café
de Flore, very good families can be seen dipping their
croissants in their coffee (which must be milky),
but they draw the line at *une tartine*, a long slice of
buttered baguette, because of meltdown. Gené says
that the croissant dunker should begin by soaking the
two extremities, working to the middle. Later, he can
advance to a brioche, which requires constant
attention in case of disintegration.

Nadine de Rothschild, who has produced a book
and a video on aristocratic table manners, claims
mopping up gravy and dunking are equally impolite.
In Britain, there is little scholarship so far on the
subject, beyond the analysis of the survival times of a
McVities' digestive biscuit in tea or coffee.

Here, dunking has impeccable historical and literary roots: Proust was an inveterate dunker, drowning up to three croissants a day in his *café-au-lait*, and the famous madeleine was soggy with lime-blossom tea. The madeleine is particularly suited to tea – perhaps a light Ceylon, or First Flush Darjeeling. Unfortunately, Typhoo acts like an acid bath on the delicate cake – *a la recherche du lumps perdu*.

COOKING AT
THE RITZ

Juniper berries and beurre blanc

As Anthelme Brillat-Savarin, France's 18th-century foodie, once remarked: 'Gastronomic knowledge is necessary for all men, for it increases the sum of pleasure which is their destiny.'

Taking this sensible advice, I enrol for the afternoon at the Ritz Escoffier[1] school of gastronomy. The Ritz, which is linked to the hotel, and its rival the Cordon Bleu school[2], are where young English girls of a certain standing used to go after finishing school, along with chefs and restaurateurs. Both schools still cater for professionals, but now have one-day demonstrations for 'enlightened amateurs' – those with great love but limited time for gastronomy.

Between 3pm and 5.30pm the chef cooks a three-course meal, revealing techniques, ways to cheat, and food history as he goes along, with English translations. My class is in regional cooking from Alsace-Lorraine and begins with *Croquettes Jurassiennes* (croquettes with Jura cheese), *Pavé de Sandre à l'Alsacienne et son Beurre Légèr au Genièvre* (Alsatian pike-perch fillets with juniper berry butter sauce) and *Savarin* (rum baba).

The demonstration, or more performance, is in a white room tiled with a mural of game birds. The audience perches on little blue chairs, before a stainless steel counter – the stage. The chef's every action – such as slicing onions at full speed without looking down at his knife – is reflected in a huge tilted mirror above the counter.

My neighbour is a well-rounded Frenchman whose wife has given him a week's classes at the Ritz as a birthday present. He says our chef, Monsieur Barroyer, 'not only knows his onions, but knows precisely where they were grown'. Behind us, Japanese débutantes and a posse of wives of American heart surgeons take careful notes on their Ritz clipboards.

M. Barroyer is himself from Lorraine, and grouches as he stirs that the food from the north east of France is under-appreciated. 'My ingredients here are as they are, not elaborate and overworked,' he sniffs.

He begins in the middle of a meal, parading the sauerkraut with which he will stuff perfect squares of pike-perch. 'Not originally from Alsace, you know,' he says munching a handful of the pickled cabbage. 'From China, in fact.'

He turns to the sugar syrup for soaking the sponge baba. He pares a lemon and orange perfectly with a potato-peeler to give the syrup flavour, and then throws in a teabag. 'The tea adds a certain freshness, a tartness – nowadays you don't want a sickly sugar taste.'

His assistant asks if there are any questions. 'Yes, how long does it take to become a chef?' asks an American wife-of. M. Barroyer is crushing: 'Time has no meaning for a great chef. You cannot learn love and sensitivity at a cookery school, you can only learn the basic techniques.'

He ambidextrously whips the rubber dough for the baba into shape, and we watch his arm muscles bulge. 'You can do this at home with a mixer,' he says to the weaklings in the audience. He says the baba was conceived when a king of Poland objected to the dry ring of sponge and suggested pouring alcohol on it. 'The king liked his drink,' says M. Barroyer. 'He died when he took a bit too much and fell of his chair into the fire.'

The drier the baba, the better, so the sponge soaks up more liquid. The chef suggests leaving the sponge on top of a cupboard for a fortnight, covered with a cloth.

Slowly, various exquisite smells percolate the room. The *beurre blanc* with juniper mingles with rum and orange and the class begins to pant. The final result is displayed, perfectly arranged on a tablecloth with flowers. It is 5.30pm, the moment we have been waiting for. Tiny saucers are supplied, each with a tasting portion of each course. We tuck in.

1   RITZ ESCOFFIER ECOLE DE GASTRONOMIE FRANÇAISE,
        38 Rue Cambon, 1st, M Concorde, 01 43 16 31 43.
        Demonstration Fr275.
2   LE CORDON BLEU ECOLE DE CUISINE ET PATISSERIE,
        15th, 8 Rue Léon Delhomme, M Vaugirard, 01 53 68 22 50.
        Demonstration Fr 220.

❝Very fond of the *Figaro* women's page on Saturdays, which harks back to another time. It is entirely concerned with food, despite being titled *La Vie au Féminin*. Each week, a seasonal product is fêted: 'The sardine: king of the fishes'; 'The leek: a green goddess'; 'The crayfish: how it runs, how it runs!'

Laughably complex recipes are couched in the highest literary tones. Under 'New potatoes: they're worth their weight in gold!', the merits of the Noirmoutier potato (no mere tattie at £7 a kilo) were discussed: 'The glorious Noirmoutier is an aristocrat. Not some court-appointed peer-come-lately, but more a Rohan or a La Rochefoucauld [very old money]. The Noirmoutier is to the potato family what Château Lafite is to Bordeaux: the very best. If he'd tasted it, Baudelaire would not have succumbed to opium, and Verlaine would have given up absinthe.'

"In the asparagus season the debate rages in the Rue du Bac greengrocer's: 'The white is the most popular,' says Madame in her checked pinny, 'but the violet tipped has its partisans. Then there are others who only swear by the green.' As any Parisian knows, asparagus is not a vegetable: it is art. Manet offered his still life *Une botte d'asperges* to a buyer for Fr800. When the man paid Fr1,000, Manet painted a single asparagus, *L'asperge*, and sent it over with a note: 'One was missing from your bunch.'

WINE

For the bibulous learner

Although France is more than self-assured about the quality of its wines, tongue-scarring stuff is still served in many cafés. This is why the French drink so much Kir as an apéritif: the *crème de cassis*, or blackcurrant liqueur, kills the bleachy taste of cheap white wine. A great improvement on this is the recent revival of the Cardinal, which couples *crème de mûre* (bramble) with chilled light red wine, like Gamay or Sancerre, and is kinder to the palate.

For a superior glass, however, the sensible Parisian attends his local wine bar, particularly at lunchtime, when food – especially cheese – is better than café fare. Wine bar owners have a reputation to keep. Their vintages are carefully chosen, often specializing in a specific area like the Rhône, Bordeaux or the Loire, and customers and owners can indulge in pretentious and useful discussion of each bottle.

For those who are not wine buffs, a few hours' work at the zinc of a wine bar can result in knowledge useful for purchasing a case. Many Paris wine bars also sell wine from their cellars by the bottle or dozen to take home, which often beats making wild guesses in an off-licence.

Le Rubis,[1] an ancient institution just down from

the Opéra, is your traditional wine bar, with sawdust on the floors and barrels on which to stand your glass. After tasting, you can also buy bottles to take home. It is noisy, amusing and packed, particularly when the hangoverish Beaujolais Nouveau is launched in November and it seems to require a constant police presence.

All over Paris, it seems, there are branches of L'Ecluse[2] wine bar – a reliable chain with good wines which lacks eccentricity, but is a step up from falling into the nearest café. Perhaps the best-decorated wine bar in the city is the Clown Bar[3] which was built next door to the old Cirque d'Hiver building, and is exquisitely tiled with circus and clown motifs. The wine is served in generous glasses, with much discussion.

On the Left Bank, the Bistro des Augustins[4] is charming, with an art deco bar and lighting, delicious sourdough Pain Poilâne, runny cheeses and homemade puddings. Again, wines can be tried and taken away.

Although French-style wine bars invaded Britain long ago, revenge has been taken by Englishman Mark Williamson, who opened Willi's Wine Bar[5] in the business district 19 years ago, and its offshoot Juveniles more recently. Willi's has superb food and a cellar which varies from the offbeat to the grand. Wines by the glass, which you wish was larger, cost from Fr16 to Fr70. The bar specializes in wines from the Rhône, the south west and Provence and, unlike many French wine bars, it does stock a range of what the owner describes as 'fun wines' from Italy, Spain and California. It also has an extraordinary range of sherries, 'a rarity here,' says Williamson who has been fighting the native assumption that sherry is *pas le goût français*.

Williamson searches carefully for his vintages, trawling the countryside and wine salons. The specials – unlike those of many Parisian wine bars – change every day. Recently he had a fine 1993 Mersault from Pierre Morey, and a Domaine de Trevallon Cabernet Sauvignon from Provence from the same year.

Although Willi's does not sell selections from its cellar, its cheaper offshoot Juveniles[6] will supply wine by the case. There wine usually costs between Fr16 and Fr30 a glass, and is of more recent vintage.

Williamson says his clientele was mostly French until the Chunnel opened. At lunchtime, workers pour in to Willi's from the Bourse and ministries nearby. The other night at dinner, however, we were trapped at a table between four London accountants all wearing steel-rimmed spectacles, and American businessmen and women from New Jersey expertly mistranslating the menu.

Wine buying is worth every bottle, especially if you have a car, since prices are double or treble across the Channel. Aside from grabbing the bargains in the two Paris chains, Le Repaire de Bacchus and Nicolas, the wine sections of the big *périphérique* supermarkets like Carrefour are both sophisticated and economical. Then there are various grand *négociants* wine merchants, each with partic-ular shops and predilections.

Paris has a couple of remaining vineyards at Suresnes, and the famed hill of Montmartre. The Montmartre wine – not special except for the label – can be bought from the local town hall in the 18th *arrondissment*. There is even a wine museum[7] out at Passy in the arched stoned cellar of an old monastery, with ancient bottles, barrels, machines and cut-out peasants, if you like that sort of thing, with a tasting at the end. More fun for the avid learner are the courses at the Centre d'Information et de Dégustation[8] of wine. One off three-hour lectures in English including tastings (*dégustations*) are Fr410, with longer courses at Fr1,300. You can study 'The Mechanics and Principles of Tasting', 'The Nose – Aromas and Bouquet', particular regions and that essential 'Vocabulary and Picturesque Expressions for Wine Lovers'.

1   LE RUBIS, 10 Rue du Marché St Honoré, 1st, M Tuileries,
       01 42 61 03 34.
2   L'ECLUSE (Paris chain), 64 Rue François-1er, 8th, M Georges V,
       01 47 20 77 09.
3   CLOWN BAR, 114 Rue Amelot, 11th, M Filles du Calvaire,
       01 43 55 87 35.
4   BISTRO DES AUGUSTINS, 39 Quai des Grands-Augustins, 6th, M St
       Michel, 01 43 54 41 65.
5   WILLI'S, 13 Rue de Petits-Champs, 1st, M Pyramides, 01 42 61 05 09.
6   JUVENILES, 47 Rue de Richelieu, 1st, M Pyramides,
       01 42 97 46 49.
7   MUSEE DU VIN, 5 Square Charles Dickens, 16th, M Passy,
       01 45 25 63 26.
8   CENTRE D'INFORMATION ET DE DEGUSTATION DU VIN,
       30 Rue de la Sablière, 14th, 01 45 45 32 20.

"The Harvest Festival takes place in October in the last vineyard in Paris: on the rue St Vincent on the hill of Montmartre. Le Clos de Montmartre can be bought at the town hall in the 18th arrondissement, and is said to be 'long undrinkable but now improving'. The grapes are often gathered during Level 3 pollution alerts and the vintage is presumably filtered through a catalytic converter.

The 'godmother' of one year's Montmartre harvest was the actress Sophie Marceau. She was not the best

publicity cheerleader, refusing to be photographed
with the over-excited mayor, although eventually she
agreed to pose alone with a bottle. She was publicity
sensitive because someone had written a pop song
eulogizing *Les Seins* [breasts] *de Sophie Marceau*. She
sued the songwriter on behalf of her breasts.

"One summer night after we had been recruited as
dining companions by food writer, Paul Levy in the
Carré des Feuillants restaurant (14, Rue de
Castiglione, 1st, M Concorde, 01 42 86 82 82), we
were led down into the warren of stone cellars below.
The cold entered not just our light clothes but our
bones as we walked the black corridors filled with
dusty bottles. The party of explorers, including the
Michelin two-star chef Alain Dutournier, had dined
spectacularly but nothing compared with the cellars of
the former convent which reached deep into the layers
of Paris's history. On one wall behind racks of 30-
year-old wines the words 'Jean, 1856' had been
painstakingly scraped into the stone, along with the
graffiti of other prisoners who had fallen foul of
Napoleon III and met with dank incarceration.

M. Dutournier observed our shivering discomfort
with a wicked eye and said he would not be surprised
if his wine cellars had been used over time not just as
prisons but torture chambers, as we slid past caged
Sauternes from the 1950s, gone pink with age. Then
the chef opened a series of chained and locked metal
doors and we entered the innermost sanctum. 'This
was the Gestapo hideout,' said M. Dutournier. The tiny
room was mostly taken up by a Heath Robinson-style

air-conditioning machine. Some poor lackey pedalled a bicycle to work a pump bringing fresh air through metal ducts from the street. There was also a water tap for Nazi refreshment during a long siege.

'And this,' said M. Dutournier, opening a metal door, 'was the Gestapo lavatory.' It has become a Jewish *piéce de resistance*, in both senses. 'In revenge, I keep the Mouton-Rothschild here.'

CAFÉ
DE FLORE

Not for starving artists

In the interests of research, I am spending a day in August working in the Café de Flore[1] – it had to be the Flore, what with the literary inheritance of Sartre and de Beauvoir, not forgetting Michael O'Mahoney, who does the scripts for the American TV series *Highlander* upstairs.

I'm also trying to replicate the piece by experimental writer Georges Perec: *An attempt to exhaust a Parisian place*. For three days in October 1974, Perec lurked in cafés in the Place St Sulpice, noting down 'what is generally unremarked'. It's brilliantly dull: 'The bells of St Sulpice stop ringing (was it vespers?). A 63 goes by almost empty. Night, winter: unreal aspect of the passers-by. A man carrying carpets. A lot of people, a lot of shadows, a 63 empty; the ground is shining, a 70 full, the rain seems heavier. It is six-ten. Sound of horns; start of traffic jam . . . I drink a *gentiane de Salers*.'

Here's the 1998 version, without the bus timetable: 9am. Settle at desk, a red banquette indoors with prime people views. Order milky coffee, delivered in pot: Fr28 poorer. They don't do a *gentiane de Salers*, whatever that is. Dump contents of 'office' – plastic bag – on table: mulch of cuttings, hefty Perec bio and novel (unread), old notebooks. Looks of disgust. Borrow pen from waiter. Chew it.

10am. Can't concentrate. De Beauvoir wrote whole novels here. Keep eavesdropping on other Eurotrash (no Parisians in Paris in August) and noting down their restaurant recommendations. In de Beauvior's time 'the regulars were neither wholly Bohemian nor wholly bourgeois . . . They lived on unspecified private incomes, from hand to mouth, or on their expectations.' Now, the Flore clientele is just plain rich. I feel duty-bound to order something hourly, when the waiter curls his lip and single eyebrow menacingly and says: '*Oui, madame?*' when I haven't spoken. But an espresso – which'll set you back Fr6 at my local zinc – costs Fr23. The only thing cheaper is the Fr10 hard-boiled egg. The combination is economic, but stomach churning.

11.30am. Pen shaking from caffeine. People look at me pityingly as though I've been stood up. Keep on reading. Am shocked to discover Perec lived in the Rue du Bac. On our block! You may have forgotten who Perec was. He's the man who wrote the novel without ever using the letter 'e', very demanding in French. In the 1960s, Perec's idea of ecstasy was to sit in cafés with his mates holding E-less conversations. If you try it in our own idiom, you'll find initial fascination turns to irritation and soon agony, until you losE it.

Flick through Perec's other novel *Life: A User's Manual* which is the story of dozens of (somewhat) connected lives in a Paris apartment block. Discover book has index. Look up my favourite subject.

Perec's concierge, the widowed Madame Nochère,

is 'a tiny rather plump, voluble and obliging woman'. She doesn't correspond to the typical stairwell dragon. 'She's not mean or petty . . . She does not deliver hoarse-throated harangues against house pets, and does not rage against people emptying dustbins in the morning or growing flowers in pots on their balconies.' I nod. Some time ago, my concierge banned my prized geraniums for lowering the tone of the building.

12.15pm. Go to loo. Bet they didn't have the whizround seat covers in Sartre's day. Return and order Diet Coke. At Fr34 you'd have to be Danielle Steele to afford to work here full time.

But back to concierges. It took a few days for us to notice, but there was a visible lifting of tension in our apartment block last week. People were daringly parking their bikes in the prams-only section, putting their rubbish out at all hours, and illegally singing on the stairs. There were no dawn raids with the mail, when one had to answer the door in a bed-crumpled Johnny Hallyday T-shirt. No longer were there notices taped to the lift floor saying: 'Would whoever made this mess kindly clean it up.' Yes, the concierge was on holiday.

We remaining residents nearly held a celebratory barbie in the courtyard. Lurking downstairs is normally against regulations. Even when my son had chickenpox and could not be paraded in public, he was banned from silently riding his plastic tractor round the yard. Now, for the first time, we hung out down there, talking.

The decadence was not to last. At 8 o'clock one morning, there was a sharp knock, and a henna-haired woman of military bearing, her faced gashed by blood-red lipstick, threw the *Figaro* in to us. 'I am the replacement concierge for the month,' she boomed.

'Oh how nice. Have you worked before as a concierge in Paris?' I asked. 'No. I'm from Béziers,' she said, rippling her biceps. 'I'm a psychiatric nurse.'

1.10pm. Flore is packed for lunch, and my paper mountain and I are taking up two seats. Resolutely avoid waiter's eye. Realize have only brought a Fr100 note and some change, and have been bankrupted by two coffees, a Coke and an egg. Consider leaving remaining Fr5 as tip, but spend it instead on bus to better place: the office.

1   CAFÉ DE FLORE, 172 Boulevard St Germain, 6th, M St Germain, 01 45 48 55 26.

“In 1685, Louis XIV's secretary wrote to the chief of police: 'The king has been informed that in several places in Paris where one can drink coffee, there are meetings of all sorts of people, particularly foreigners. On this subject, His Majesty orders me to ask you whether we should put a stop to this in future.'

Felicitously, the chief of police filed that letter in his wastebasket. Had he clamped down on those caffeinated seditionaries, we might never have seen the Revolution, the rise of the literary café, or the post-modern outbreak, literature about the literary café.

Two books have recently been published: one on the Deux Magots, another on the lit caff in general. The author of Les Cafés Littéraires, Gérard-Georges Lemaire, admits there was little to beat the 'golden triangle' in St Germain of the Flore, the Deux Magots and

Brasserie Lipp, now a Bermuda triangle bent on
sucking up tourists. But Le Procope along the road is
really the heavyweight amongst caffs, boasting, over
three centuries, Voltaire, Beaumarchais and Rousseau,
then Marat, Danton and Robespierre, finishing with
Hugo, George Sand and Balzac. Nowadays Le Procope
is over-restored and intellectually vacant – more decaf
than caff.

RESTAURANTS

Finding the best and latest

Much as I would like to, I cannot disclose my top 20 Paris restaurants, a list honed through years of suffering and diligence, because it would be sure to be out of date in six months after publication. Of course the city has its grand old standards – the three-star Alain Ducasse and Taillevent; the beautiful brasseries like Bofinger and the Coupole where the decor matters more than the food; and the unchanging corner bistros – but nowadays the British diner wants more.

Since the Conran-led restaurant revolution has left us with discerning palates and strong opinions on restaurant design, the fact that food is French will no longer suffice. For the first time, the British are no longer merely grateful just to be somewhere foreign eating cassoulet, *steak frites*, a *choucroute garni* or fish in *beurre blanc*. They expect innovation, value for money and fresh rather than overcooked vegetables. Thus it has become necessary to trawl the French restaurant recommendations and book ahead for the perfect meal. Here, we select the best guides to restaurants and bistros.

Way ahead of anything else in English (and possibly in French), in terms of wide coverage and value for money, is the regularly updated *Time Out Guide to Eating and Drinking in Paris*.[1] It's Fr35 at newsagents, and it is sensitive to British and American tastes. The sections include bistros, *haute cuisine*, trendy, fish, budget and vegetarian (not a Gallic speciality) as well as cafés and bars. For up-to-the-minute news, check the Time Out section in the weekly listings' magazine *Pariscope*.

The other new invader from abroad is the *Zagat Survey*[2] from New York, written by the punters, for the punters. Although it tends to favour the grand over the innovative at the moment, it is generally reliable and a convenient pocket size. There is both an English and a French version, updated yearly.

That staple, the *Michelin Guide*, is pretty useless unless you are profoundly rich. Then, any old two or three star restaurant will suit, but for those who loathe pomp and prices, the Michelin merely lists the addresses of middle-range restaurants without comment.

If your French is up to it, try tackling one of the specialist Paris guides, since food language is not taxing, and most provide symbols indicating their favourites. The *Pudlo Guide*[3], out every autumn, lists 1,320 eating establishments, as well as the best food shops. It is divided by *arrondissement*, and details atmosphere, some of the dishes and an average price. There are little plate symbols to indicate food quality, and knife and fork symbols to indicate the grandness and comfort of the restaurant.

Every so often there is a boxed entry titled *Coup de Coeur* – restaurants the author adores that year. The *Pudlo* also has its *carnet noir*, or black book, for restaurants which have failed to come up to scratch. 'Charming decor but mediocre cooking,' it despairs of Le Coupe Chou in the 5th, and credits La Timonerie with 'silliest meal of the year'.

Some food critics complain, however, that some *Pudlo* entries have changed little since last year, and there are occasional errors. Another school favours the *Lebey Guides*[4] – the restaurant guide appears in the autumn, the bistro guide in February. With only 800 addresses listed, the restaurant guide is one of the most reliable, and gives one to three Eiffel Tower symbols for quality, as well as special mentions for good coffee and bread. Each entry has a partial list of the menu, as well as the last meal eaten by M. Lebey and his researchers. M. Lebey is strict – 150 of last year's restaurants were axed from the guide, and replaced by 120 new ones.

The *Gault Millau*[5] guide grades by marks out of 20 and chefs' *toques* or hats. The list is mostly reliable, though not as long as the *Pudlo* or *Lebey*, and tends to the grand. Red titles, however, indicate good deals or *bon rapport qualité prix*.

In general, the French guides pay almost no attention to decoration and atmosphere, focusing on the food, under near-fluorescent light if possible. It's a different sensibility. Then there is the question of favouritism; we know Michelin sends in anonymous inspectors, but some of the other food critics from newspapers and guides are instantly recognizable, and expect fawning attention. The owner of my delicious local bistro found himself unlisted in one of the guides. He realized he'd made the cardinal error of asking the Great Gastronomic Critic to pay his bill.

1   THE TIME OUT GUIDE TO EATING AND DRINKING IN PARIS.
2   THE ZAGAT SURVEY.
3   LE PUDLO DE PARIS GOURMAND, Ramsay.

4   LE GUIDE LEBEY DES RESTAURANTS DE PARIS, Albin Michel.

5   GUIDE GAULT MILLAU PARIS.

Both French and English guides are available in English bookshops in Paris such as Brentanos or W.H. Smith.

"Paris restaurants are jockeying for the coveted Society for the Protection of Egg Mayonnaise awards. The Society's president is the critic Claude Lebey, who wears sock garters and takes the ASOM (*Association pour Sauvegarder l'Oeuf Mayonnaise*) diploma most seriously: 'By defending egg mayonnaise – the emblem of bistro cooking – we also defend the traditional bistro.'

Not only the menus, he laments, but bistros' classic red banquettes and smoke-yellowed walls are at risk from the encroaching Philippe Starck ethos. M. Lebey fears that the eggy starter may fall into desuetude along with pigs' trotters and noses, veal headcheese, blood-boltered sausages and other fatty items. 'The threat is not to *cuisine de terroir* [native cooking], but to *cuisine de trottoir* [pavement cooking].'

This is art, not hard-boiled with Hellmann's, so what makes the perfect egg mayonnaise? 'Ah, that would take half an hour to explain,' sighed M. Lebey. I gave him two minutes. 'The lettuce leaves should be whole, alluring, providing a crunchy background. Add three halved eggs, boiled enough but not too much, perhaps ten minutes. They must have the right consistency, as must the mayonnaise. It should cover, yet not be too liquid, rather like a tablecloth draping the eggs. It is far from simple.'

"French *Vogue* has brought out its food guide, with a new section: Restaurants with Flattering Light. This list has been long-awaited in Paris, where popular fluorescent lighting allows a microscopic examination of one's swordfish carpaccio, but does little for human flesh over 30.

Benoît is recommended for 'a quality of light particularly adapted to beauties in the style of Emma Bovary. Fine, lightly rosy skins are at their best here, especially with the air conditioning'. Ladurée has lighting that is, 'ideal when one is feeling a touch pale and low.'

No mistress should be without this Chanel-bag-sized guide, for it also includes places to avoid during a *liaison dangereuse*.

PARIS
ON FOOT

WALKING TOURS

Dr Guillotin and the sheep

Paris Walking Tours[1] began as a husband-and-wife hobby with a couple of simple walks, but is now a full-time business employing other English guides and offering two walks most days, three on Sundays. Their most popular tours are two in the Marais, one named 'Mansions, mistresses and murderers', the other 'Saints and sinners'. They offer a dozen others, lasting up to two hours, including the Paris Sewers, the Latin Quarter, Montmartre Village and the more obscure Art Nouveau Walk in the 16th *arrondissement*. Other companies offer walks – details of which are in the Time Out English section of *Pariscope* each week – but Paris Walking Tours is the largest and most reliable company, whatever the weather. French language walks are advertised in *Pariscope* and the *Figaro*. Although creating your own tour is possible – *Paris Step by Step*[2] is a good walking guidebook – the guided version chucks in instant history, literature and local knowledge of hidden courtyards and back streets. I tested the St Germain des Prés tour, since it was on my own doorstep and the streets were familiar.

You meet the guide at the lion fountains of St Sulpice. Your fellow walkers are a motley crew, tending more to middle age, but they're generally respectful, and don't ask stupid questions. The guides themselves have researched their patch, and can usually handle requests for more detail. In St Sulpice church, the tour concentrates on Delacroix's murals and the interesting fact that the south tower is 16 feet shorter than the north, and a great deal less ornate, since building was halted by the Revolution.

From there, you wander up Rue Bonaparte (home of Catherine Deneuve) to St Germain itself and the church, once an abbey which covered the entire patch between Rue St Benoît and Rue Jacob, parts of which date back to 542. The main church was consecrated in the twelfth century, when it still had a wooden roof. Inside, the original architecture was painted in the nineteenth century by Hippolyte Flandrin to give what we would now describe as a Jocasta Innes look – faded red, blue and grey-green designs painted on the pillars and ceilings.

During the Revolution, the abbey was used to store explosives, and two of its grand towers were blown up. The revolutionaries also executed the 316 monks remaining on the premises, in what is now a pleasant garden. Descartes is buried here – in full now, since his head was stolen from his original burial place in Stockholm, and travelled widely until it was later reunited with his body in St Germain.

The walk also covers the Café de Flore, Les Deux Magots and the Brasserie Lipp and their one-time customers from Surrealists to Sartre, and Trotsky to Chou En-lai. The latest St Germain story is, of course, the gentrification taking place, with an outbreak of Cartier, Armani, Conran and Prada in the once-bohemian quarter.

Still following the old abbey walls, now regular streets, you go to the Delacroix museum in his old studio

off the Place de Furstenburg, and pass where Alexandre
Dumas had his printer, the apartment where Richard
Wagner lived for a year, the scroggy two-storey house in
Paris's narrowest street where Racine died, and George
Sand's house. 'She was famous for wearing trousers,' the
guide tells the Americans. Depending on the intelligence
and size of the crowd – usually up to 15 people – the tour
is forced to vary in complexity.

Up at the top of Rue Bonaparte, there is the
Academie des Beaux Arts, still a working art school, but
the tour sneaks into the courtyard, church and great hall, if
it is open. On the Rue des Beaux Arts opposite is L'Hôtel,
where Oscar Wilde died in unhappy exile. The tour finish-
es with the building that houses Picasso's studio in the Rue
des Grands Augustins, although other tours of the area like
'The French Revolution and the Latin Quarter' will take
you to the Passage St André de Commerce, filled with little
shops and cafés, where there are two good finds. Above the
houses pokes one of the remaining towers of the original
city wall, which then excluded the village of St Germain.
Nearby is one of the finest courtyards in Paris, the Cour de
Rohan, with three interlocking plant-draped squares, one
of which was used by Dr Guillotin when testing his new
contraption, the guillotine, on various unlucky sheep.

1   PARIS WALKING TOURS, Fr60, 01 48 09 21 40, website at
        http://ourworld.compuserve.com/homepages/ParisWalking.
2   PARIS STEP BY STEP by Christopher Turner, Pan Books: walking
        routes through Paris.

❝This is the last chapter in The Fall of St Germain, a
saga of the dark forces of capitalism crushing the
lackadaisical resistance of literary bohemianism. We
bring this report to you from the mezzanine café in
the new Emporio Armani store, which we secretly
like. The French call it 'le look Zen': we call it
magnolia paint. We might as well be in SoHo, New
York, rather than the corner of the Boulevard St
Germain. At any moment, we feel J.F.K. Junior and
Caroline Bessette Kennedy will join us. We are drinking a decaf cappuccino – a drink we wouldn't be seen
dead with in a real Paris café – and observing the rich
wildlife.

Rich underplays it. These people are oozing dosh
and squeezing £5,000 Armani suits as though they
were ripe melons, and just as cheap. They have logos
on their ears (Paloma Picasso), their eyes (Armani),
their bags (Prada, still) and their shoes (Gucci). Their
platinum Amexes flit from Vuitton by the Café de
Flore, across the road to Cartier, which has replaced
the music shop, and past the former bookshop which
will soon be Dior Homme. They end with a cocktail at
the Fashionbar or the Deux Magots, which used to
claim on its menu it was *le rendez-vous de l'élite
intellectuelle*. Now it's merely a backdrop in a sex-'n'-
shopping blockbuster.

S.O.S. St Germain, a pressure group of raddled
old Left-Bank intellectuals and singers, believes the
replacement of the sleazy all-night 'le Drugstore' by
Armani is the last straw, but dare not say so, since
Giorgio has donated part of his first three days' takings
to the renovation fund for the St Germain church

tower. The satirical *Canard Enchainé* newspaper
suggests the money should go towards stained-glass
windows depicting long-dead saints: St Simone de
Beauvoir and St Jean-Paul Sartre.

" The Café Mabillion – once a run-down student
and tourist dive with rickety tables and medieval
bathrooms – has had a makeover, with red velvet
chairs, purple and pink walls, and 1950s-style lights
and chrome. The owners say they wanted to 'give St
Germain back its literary youth and bohemian
nightlife' by opening 24 hours. Changing the image is
one thing. Changing the clientele is another. Just
before midnight one weekday night, the best table on
the street was occupied by a genteel grande dame of at
least 80 years, who had made a *crème brûlée* and stiff
drink last for nearly two hours before wobbling off
cheerfully on her stick.

NEW RÉPUBLIQUE

Trend central

Easy come, easy go. In the 1970s and early 1980s, the Marais rose from obscurity to become Paris's trendiest patch. Then it was eclipsed in the 1990s by the younger Bastille, as Jean Paul Gaultier, Kenzo and co turned old warehouses into loft spaces amid an outbreak of fresh bars. Now, the action for the next century has moved to the north of the 11th *arrondissement*, above the Bastille and around République. In Rue Oberkampf alone, 20 new bars and bistros have opened in the last three years.

Any area that is up and coming must also have parts which are down and dying, and this is the case with what one might call the New République. Between the designer flower shops, postmodern and renovated cafés, and ironic merchandisers of 1950's, kitsch, there are still plenty of stores selling orange plastic buckets or tripe.

The 11th *arrondissement* is almost a tourist-free zone, and there is still an edginess in the air. It was here, after all, that the French Revolution began when the Sans Culottes from Rue Faubourg St Antoine stormed the Bastille. Those working classes have now been joined by thousands of Jewish, Turkish and Arab immigrants, followed closely by a series of exotic little restaurants.

The main drags of the New République area are Rue Oberkampf, Rue Amelot, Rue Jean Pierre Timbaud, Rue Faubourg du Temple at Belleville, and for greenery and calm, the Canal St Martin – where everyone is vying to convert industrial lofts. The explorer needs to have a sharp eye for the *branché* among the ordinary.

Starting on the Rue Amelot, there is the spectacular Cirque d'Hiver building. The circus is ringed with friezes of horses and men, by sculptors including Pradier, on a terra-cotta background. It was built by Napoleon III to buy admiration in proper bread-and-circuses style from the stroppy working classes in the 11th. The circus has gone, although Alexander McQueen did stage his fashion show here. Next door, however, the atmosphere remains in the Bar du Cirque and the Clown Bar, with its wonderful tiled walls showing circus acts. It also does good Kir.

Nearby, there is Au Camelot[1], a kitschy-Provence looking restaurant which provides five stunning courses for F140. The catch is that there is absolutely no choice – you eat what is on that day's blackboard. It has about ten over-lit scruffy tables, and is run by Didier Varnier, a defector from the two-star Crillon.

From there, the explorer can potter up Rue Oberkampf, past the exuberant flower shop, Sarah's Persian restaurant with a *plat du jour* at F35, along to Lulu Berlu at number 27, where the worst junk of the French 1950s is available. There are Michelin men glow-lights and a plastic electric Citroen DX. At 25 is the art deco building housing Balagan, and bar-restaurant which supplies its customers with armchairs, tiddlywinks and chess.

If you felt like taking up temporary residence in the area, on the nearby Rue de Malte, there is a World Gym and various hotels catering for all grades of humanity, from the frighteningly basic one-star fleapits at F180 up to the grander Croix de Malte[2], at F600 a double room, with modern paintings and crisp rooms in blue, green and white.

Across Avenue de la République, still on Oberkampf, there is the warehoused-sized Café Charbon[3], now impossibly packed on weekend nights, but an acceptable place to eat and read the paper during the day. Charbon is a cavernous old café which has been gently restored, enabling models, writers and pseudo-intellectuals to be seen in the best light. It often has a DJ after 10pm, making it half-café, half-club. Along similar lines is the Mécano Bar[4] just down the street, with a *pression* beer at an economical Fr12.

One does not come here to eat, but merely to be. However, style revolutionaries may dine until early morning in many of the bistros along Oberkampf which have colonized old ironmongers' and drapers' shops. The Brazilian restaurant Favela Chic[5] spills out into the street and is particularly good value, a cantina with fresh specials, the traditional caipirinha cocktail and a curious Mojito made from rum and fresh mint. Roseanne, the owner, is about to open a Favela Chic Hotel too.

Later on, the citizens of the New République repair to the old La Java[6] dance hall, now a Latino haunt, for salsa, tango, or a certain amount of mambo.

1   AU CAMELOT, 50 Rue Amelot, 11th, M Filles du Calvaire,
    01 43 55 54 04.
2   CROIX DE MALTE HOTEL, 5 Rue de Malte, 11th, M Oberkampf,
    01 48 05 09 36.
3   CAFE CHARBON, 109 Rue Oberkampf, 11th, M Parmentier,
    01 43 57 55 13.
4   MECANO BAR, 99 Rue Oberkampf, 11th, M Parmentier,
    01 40 21 35 28,

5   FAVELA CHIC, 131 Rue Oberkampf, 11th M Belleville,
       01 43 57 15 47.
6   LA JAVA, 105 Rue Faubourg du Temple, 11th, M Belleville,
       01 42 02 20 52.

"Costs an amazing £5 million a year for the upkeep of the Luxembourg Gardens. Initially, it puzzled me that cutting grass and lopping a few trees would be so expensive, but after months of careful, near-daily observation I realize: it's the espaliering, stupid. Never before have fruit trees and geometry been so closely aligned.

The Luxembourg has hundreds of varieties of apples, pears, apricots and plums, all raised under more military than horticultural discipline. The unconventional offshoot meets with instant reprisals. At any time, at least three uniformed gardeners stand armed and combat-ready. Trees may grow in 'bobbin, pyramid, palm and double U' formations, or else face the consequences. The garden even offers 20 free lessons to the public, with particular emphasis on the pear tree 'and its enemies'.

MITTERRAND'S
MEMORIALS

Monuments and mistresses tour

Like any French king, during his long reign François
Mitterrand left behind a number of monuments, not all of
which were architectural. All around Paris, there are daily
reminders of his public presence, from La Grande Arche
at La Défense, to the new book-shaped Bibliothèque
de France and the Louvre Pyramid. And all around the
Left Bank, there are reminders of his spectacularly
complex private life, in the homes of his two mistresses
and wife.

The tour of Mitterrand's monuments and mistresses
would be difficult to complete in a day, so scattered are the
sights, but any visitor cannot fail to pass a few incidentally.
Here we provide a guide to the major works, the great ego
and, as far as possible, the specific street numbers of the
various residences.

The Bibliothèque Mitterrand down by the Gare
d'Austerlitz is the last of *tonton's* (uncle's) *grands travaux*.
Although erected faster and more efficiently than the
new British Library, its unsurpassed ugliness and inconve-
nience for pedestrians have not proved popular. Architect
Dominique Perrault's four towers, which are supposed to

resemble open books, already have ugly blinds hanging at the windows to keep out the blinding light. The basin between the towers is filled with full-size fir trees imported from Scandinavia, but humans are not allowed to promenade in the garden, because the trees are held in place by dozens of guy ropes.

Former President Mitterrand's other Scandinavian import was more successful – his long affair with Paris-based Swedish journalist Christina Forsne, which resulted in his supposed nine-year-old son, Ravn. Unlike the great 'coming out' of Mitterrand's illegitimate daughter Mazarine and second family in *Paris-Match* and at his funeral, the presence of Ravn was kept fairly secret. Mitterrand was a regular visitor in the 1980s to Mme Forsne's apartment on the Ile St Louis. After the birth of her child, she moved to 4 Rue Rollin in the Latin Quarter when she was not staying at the Elysée Palace. Now, however, Mme Forsne has moved back to Sweden and has written her memoirs of the Mitterrand years *Don't You Love Life?* from there.

It is a short walk from Rue Rollin towards the river and 22 Rue de Bièvre, the apartment with a garden where Mitterrand conducted the legitimate part of his private life, usually lunching there on Sundays with his wife Danielle and his family. From there, you can take one of Mitterrand's favourite strolls along the *bouquinistes* – the bookstalls lining the Seine – and pick up one of the 50 or so Mitterrand biographies available, or perhaps a remaindered copy of *Premier Roman*, his daughter Mazarine's first novel, about – surprisingly – a young Parisian who goes to the best schools and has an obsessive relationship with her powerful father.

From the *bouquinistes*, it is but a short step to the

Louvre. There, there is perhaps the most popular symbol of Mitterrand's era, I. M. Pei's glass Pyramid in the Cour Napoléon, which began as controversial, but is now so much part of the city that it is used as a Paris symbol on the cover of guidebooks, instead of the clichéd Eiffel Tower.

Many other great projects are worth seeing only if you have good reason to go there: the Finance Ministry at Bercy, concerts at La Cité de la Musique, and performances at the Opéra Bastille. The new Opera was criticized as an 'aesthetic error' when it was built, but it has served to revitalize the area round the Bastille. Unfortunately, the building has coped badly with ten years of weather and pollution, and tiles started crashing down on the pavements. It is presently covered in safety nets until the cladding is fixed. Roman emperors never had these irritations.

Most of Mitterrand's monuments can be seen in a panoramic view from the top of the Grande Arche at La Défense, an ironic take on the Arc de Triomphe. The Danish architect Johan Otto von Spreckelsen was commissioned for the project, but died before completion of the arch, which is slightly squint, 112m high, and covered in white marble.

From the arch, there is a clear view of the Eiffel Tower, in the shadow of which lies Mitterrand's final resting and trysting place, a traditional apartment and office at 9 Avenue Frédéric Le Play. Crowds still come here on the anniversary of the great socialist's death on 8 January, bringing single red roses. His deathbed photographs from there were bizarrely published in *Paris-Match*, public till the end. His long term mistress, the Musée d'Orsay curator Anne Pingeot and mother of Mazarine, lived in an adjoining state-financed flat also at number 9. Mazarine, incidentally, was named after Rue Mazarine in the 6th *arrondissement*, where her mother and Mitterrand first began their affair.

"Decide to walk the two miles from the Left Bank to the office at the Opéra – after all, it's your textbook Paris morning: the sunlight's dancing on the Seine, on the gilded dome of the Invalides and on the gold buttons of passing heiresses. I've mapped myself a 35-minute route which will take in the Pont des Invalides, the Grand Palais, the Champs-Elysées, the Elysée Palace and the Madeleine.

Full of the joys of temporary childlessness and spring, I skip round the back of the Elysée Palace, wondering if Chirac's breakfast is as good as the canapés I enjoyed there the other week. I hear shouts and walk on. Then the long arm of the law is upon me. A gendarme taps my shoulder. 'It is illegal to walk on this pavement, Madame,' he says.

Stupidly, I argue: 'So where's the sign saying that?'

'It is forbidden,' he says, stonily. Bizarrely, you're allowed to walk on the pavement in *front* of the Elysée Palace, but not at the side. Another gendarme muscles in. He's armed with a revolver and I'm armed with a *pain au chocolat* in a paper bag. They win, and escort me to the other side of the road.

Which leads me to the question: hasn't the gendarmerie got anything less pedestrian to do? Turns out that the French have the largest police force in Europe. There are 347 police for every 100,000 citizens here, while Britain has 245. This explains Chirac's over-sensitive security and the fact that 25 gendarmes are permanently on guard at former President Mitterrand's country house at Latche – and he's dead.

GREEN SPACE

From the vegetable to the intellectual

Only in Paris could a park be described as 'intellectual', but that is what everyone says about the Parc André-Citroën[1] in the 15th. Land and water have been made to conform to an architect's dream, which is also adored by Parisians and their children. Built on the enormous site of the old Citroën factory, the park is resolutely modern, down to its glass-box greenhouses and verdant concrete bridges. The fountain-installation is hundreds of squirting holes in a tiled piazza, with the water pressure controlled randomly by computer from high to low to nothing. Its unpredictability creates a sense of fear and fun. In the summer, half-naked children run screaming through the water and balance balls on the jets. But there are also areas of Zen-like calm, like the red garden with its alleys of cherry trees and benches, the silver garden, and the mini-canals trickling by. The André-Citroën is a five-minute walk from the Métro, and a million miles from old-fashioned Haussmannian Paris.

When crowds make the Luxembourg and the Tuileries a nightmare, consider heading out to the Bois du Boulogne (best by taxi rather than Métro). There, the Parc de Bagatelle[2] takes you back in time. It was once the château of the Marquis of Hertford, and its sensibility is still English, with the best rose garden in the city, strutting peacocks and a folly with a viewpoint over the park. Along tree-shaded winding paths, you find the Orangerie, where concerts are held on summer evenings, and a restaurant.

The nearby Pré-Catelan is also pretty, particularly the Shakespeare garden[3], named after the bard since it contains an open-air theatre and plants mentioned in his plays, particularly *A Midsummer Night's Dream* – 'I know a bank whereon the wild thyme blows, – Where oxlips and the nodding violet grows – Quite over-canopied with luscious woodbine, – With sweet musk-roses and with eglantine.' Unfortunately, the Jardin Shakespeare is only opened for two half hours every afternoon by its grumpy caretaker.

Back in town, the Parc des Buttes-Chaumont[4] over-looks eastern Paris from its ancient hill. In the middle of a lake, an enormous rock is topped with a Corinthian temple. From the top, you can see the Sacré Coeur and Montmartre. Two bridges lead across, one a suspension bridge, the other the Pont des Suicides, now carefully enclosed with barriers. As Louis Aragon wrote, this bridge 'claimed victims even from passers-by who had no intention of killing themselves but were suddenly tempted by the abyss.' The park was originally something between a rubbish dump and a shanty town when Haussmann cleared it in the 1860s. Now there are fake grottoes of stalactites, a waterfall, and that delight rare in many Paris parks: no keep of the grass signs.

On a smaller scale, the French *potager*, or kitchen garden, is a thing of beauty as well as nourishment. The old *potager* of the convent on the Rue Babylone in the 7th *arrondissement* was given to the public by the nuns in honour of St Catherine Labouré,[5] who saw a vision of the Virgin on the nearby Rue du Bac. There's a barely noticeable entrance, and inside the walls there are four square green patches, one still dedicated to veg, the rest for grass-deprived Parisians to lounge and play on. The garden is not worth travelling for, but if you're shopping at the nearby Bon Marché store, it provides a calm escape. Out at Versailles, the couturier Hubert de Givenchy has redesigned Louis XVI's walled vegetable garden, and one can buy the produce at certain times of the year.

Urban gardening has become newly fashionable in Paris, and a huge emporium, Vert Vous,[6] has opened on the Left Bank to cater for the outbreak of balcony and windowbox enthusiasts, as well as Le Cèdre Rouge[7] in the Rue du Bac and at the Madeleine. However, the new wave of continental gardeners are said to be keen to see instant results: the French prefer fully grown plants, while the English plot slowly from seed.

1   PARC ANDRE-CITROEN, Rue Balard or Rue St Charles, 15th, M Javel or Balard.
2   PARC DE BAGATELLE, Route de Sèvres, Bois du Boulogne, 16th.
3   JARDIN SHAKESPEARE and PRE CATELAN, Route de Suresnes, Bois du Boulogne, 16th.
4   PARC DES BUTTES-CHAUMONT, Rue Botzaris, Rue Manin, 19th, M Buttes-Chaumont.
5   JARDIN CATHERINE LABOURE, 33 Rue de Babylone, 7th, M Sèvres-Babylone.
6   VERT VOUS, 91 Boulevard Raspail, 6th, M St Placide, 01 45 48 97 41.
7   LE CEDRE ROUGE, 116 Rue du Bac, 7th M Sèvres-Babylone, 01 42 84 84 00.
Reading: *Où trouver le calme à Paris*, Parigramme, Fr35.

"During the siege of Paris in 1870, while the
bourgeoisie were reduced to dining on exotic steaks
from the zoo, the starving poor took up an equally
exotic form of fishing. The *Paris Journal* of the time
gave this advice to those lucky enough to have a
running sewer close by: 'Take a long strong line, and a
large hook, bait with tallow, and gently agitate the rod.
In a few minutes a rat will come and smell the savoury
morsel. It will be some time before he decides to
swallow it, for his nature is cunning . . . pull strongly
and steadily. He will make convulsive jumps; but be
calm, and do not let his excitement gain on you, draw
him up, *et voilà, votre dîner*'.

This vermin-catching passage came to mind last
week, when I took the children to the nearby Jardin
Catherine Labouré for a late picnic dinner. As usual,
the kids were at that grubby, hose-down stage of the
day, while their compatriots of the posh 7th
arrondissement were still in crisp linen. Unaware of the
sartorial and social divide, my sons happily made mud
pies and chased pigeons.

I was lying on a bench in the sun with my eyes half-
shut when the screams of horror from other mothers
alerted me: '*Dégoûtant! Il a attrapé un pigeon!*' Sure
enough, my youngest son, aged one and a half, had
defied all probability and was cheerfully holding a fat
bird in a rugby tackle on the ground. He'd baited it with
some (cannibalistic?) chicken sandwich from the Hédiard
deli, and then pounced. I felt secret pride in my son's
hunting prowess as I freed the surprised pigeon, while all
round me were maternal tuts. I resisted the urge to turn
upon them and say '*Et voilà, votre dîner*'.

"The *potager* in the Jardin Catherine Labouré is immensely popular with apartment-dwellers like my son who assumed vegetables materialized by themselves in supermarket plastic bags with sell-by dates.

He was initially suspicious that people kept food underground, but then incredibly excited as we minutely observed the growth of the asparagus, artichokes and green beans throughout the summer. As the season of pollution and mellow fruitfulness commenced, the under-gardener rewarded our diligence by asking us to select some veg, and filled the entire shelf of the pram with tomatoes, beetroot, basil and *blette*, a sort of Swiss chard.

I shot home, prepared the veg beautifully and served it for lunch, thinking how educational, natural and fresh the whole experience had been. Of course, my son wouldn't touch the dirty stuff, and made it clear he saw no reason whatsoever to renege on his staple diet of baked and jelly beans.

THE MARAIS

Freebies from Sacha Finkelsztajn

When Paris visitors are irrevocably divided between culture and commerce, the Marais is the sensible solution. Those without the stamina and serious-mindedness required for shopping can be sent to the Musée Carnavalet, the Musée Picasso or Victor Hugo's house. The warring sides can meet in cafés in between – the museum-goers enriched, the shoppers impoverished.

The Marais, its name meaning marsh, is swamped with tourists at the weekends, and weekdays are preferable. Nowadays the place is gentrified like New York's SoHo – establishment trendy while the Bastille and Oberkampf are edgily trendy. However, this does ensure smart bars and restaurants, and shops which succour any fashion victim.

Any basic route through the Marais should encompass the old Jewish Rue des Rosiers, the modish Rue des Francs-Bourgeois, and the Place des Vosges, while including tangential sniffs round the side streets nearby. The Marais includes some of the finest *hôtels particuliers* – walled mansions with the grandest possible architecture. The French put a preservation order on the Marais in 1962, so the grand co-exists with rambling old apartment buildings

in the narrow streets. Every entranceway that looks faintly
open should be explored – sometimes the best glimpses of
buildings are from the private courtyards within. During
the day, many buildings leave their number-coded doors
off, and you can enter and inspect by merely pressing the
entry button.

The *hôtel* now housing the Musée Carnavalet was
built in 1544 and can be first viewed through barred gates
on the Rue des Francs-Bourgeois showing the courtyard,
arches and box hedges. Inside, the building houses the
museum of the Paris history, and is particularly good on the
Revolution and Napoleon.

A few streets north is the Musée Picasso in the Hotel
Salé, another wonderful old mansion with wrought iron
work by Giacometti. Paris acquired much of Picasso's
personal collection in lieu of death taxes, and the museum
charts each phase of his development, yet is small enough
to be tackled in an hour. The sculpture, ceramics and
temporary exhibitions of photographs or Picasso's doodles
are an added delight.

The jewel of the Marais is the Place des Vosges, a
perfect 1612 square of cream stone and red brick houses in
an arcade, all overlooking the immaculately pollarded park.
A stop is required here on the park benches, or at the
corner café Ma Bourgogne, which has heaters above the
tables in winter so that terrace life can continue.

In the south-western corner of the square is the
Musée Victor Hugo,[1] and worth visiting at F17 even for
those who loathe the author of *Les Misérables*. The views
from Hugo's old third-floor apartment over the Place des
Vosges are stunning. The typical family apartment is
spacious, with sunlight-drenched panelled rooms. The

house is miserably signposted – only the second and third floors are open to the public – the trek to the fifth only unearths the bathroom. Hugo's early photos, sketches and watercolours are on display, along with tacky posters for his novels: 'The complete works: 25 centimes per volume'.

An odd charm of the apartment – although some stuffies complain – is that it overlooks the local primary school playground, shaded by chestnut trees. During the mid-afternoon break between 3 and 3.30pm, the shouts of (well-behaved) French children fracture the static air of the museum.

Going back along the Rue des Rosiers, a bastion of Jewish tradition among the encroaching trendiness, it is important to sample the falafel and delicious breads. Sacha Finkelsztajn's delicatessen[2] – the smaller of the two shops, opposite the Jewish bookshop, is often the friendliest – is renowned for its cheesecake and eastern European pastries. The rounded and moustached proprietor forced me to taste 12 dips before I selected three tubs – a caviar of red peppers, another of aubergines, an exquisite taramasalata with dill – to take home with my poppyseed bagels. Next to me, a grande dame of slender means tasted two sorts of pastrami free, and asked for another test of the first before committing herself.

1   MUSÉE VICTOR HUGO, 6 Place des Vosges, 4th, M St Paul, 01 42 72 10 16, closed Mon.
2   SACHA FINKELSZTAJN, 27 Rue des Rosiers, 4th, M St Paul, 01 42 72 78 91, closed Wed and Sat.

“Two months it took me, yomping in the bureaucracy of city hall, to gain my Paris tennis card, which allows you on municipal courts. Not until the authorities had examined my passport, my tax bill, my electricity bill and my press card did they feel I was equipped to pay to play tennis on French soil. Had they also tested hand-to-eye co-ordination, I would have failed.

Proudly flashing my photo-ID card, I skipped down to the Luxembourg Gardens to book the court. 'Naah, no way,' sneered the jobsworth in the tennis hut. 'Ya gotta book on Minitel, ain't ya?' (I translate correctly from his French.)

'But I don't have a Minitel at home . . .'

'Not my problem, lady,' he shrugged, shutting his hatch.

The Minitel is to the Internet what hairy mammoths are to elephants (we've been reading animal books at home). It's slow, it's cumbersome, it has big hair and very little brain, and ought to be extinct. For a short time, its bouffant blonde chat-up services were fashionable – 3615 YUM, 3615 BUM and variants – but basically it's a telephone directory. I spent half an hour on the office Minitel cracking the code for the tennis section, only to be told that every court in the Luxembourg was booked for the week – and every week after that, however often I tried. I'd say it was an inside job, and it would not surprise me in the least if many of the lucky players work at city hall.

Apparently you can't fight city hall, so I decided to go private. But where might one find a tennis court in the stony wastes of Paris? I called the Gymnase Club chain. 'Go to the Jardin Atlantique in Montparnasse. We have five courts there,' they said.

How delightful, I thought. A 'Jardin Atlantique', a verdant oasis in the throbbing metropolis – why hadn't I noticed it before? I realized precisely why when I got to 25 Boulevard Vaugirard – the tennis courts were on the roof of Montparnasse railway station. Up a graffiti-pocked and piss-polluted concrete stairwell, there were indeed some plastic courts and a bit of lawn with a hopeful fountain on it, this being the *jardin*. Office buildings overshadowed the grey-faced players breathing diesel. Now, I've developed a fondness for the bizarre urbanity of it all. For Fr70 a court off-peak, who's complaining? If you hit the ball over the fence, there are chances of it ending up in Orléans at 8.15pm. Bing-bong station announcements echo through air vents, and you can blame your bad serve on vibration as the TGV leaves for Toulouse.

HEMINGWAY'S PARIS

The importance of being drunk

There is a scene is Ernest Hemingway's memoir of Paris *A Moveable Feast* where he sits in his attic room at Rue Descartes, his pen iced to a halt by the cold. He considers buying kindling and a bundle of wood at the corner shop, but worries his fire may not take and his limited money will be squandered. Instead, he walks out into the rain.

'I walked past the Lycée Henri Quartre and the ancient church of St-Etienne-du-Mont and the windswept Place du Panthéon and cut in for shelter to the right and finally came out on the lee side of the Boulevard St Michel and worked on down past it past the Cluny and the Boulevard St Germain until I came to a good café that I knew on the place St Michel.'

There, the starving artist who can't afford firewood orders *café au lait*. Then a rum St James. Then another rum. Then a dozen oysters and a carafe of dry white wine. He also hones a couple of perfect sentences, and by his words and actions conforms to every cliché now expected of an ex-pat writer in Paris.

Today, the 5th *arrondissement* where Hemingway lived in the 1920s is more the haunt of the tourist classes than working, drinking and writing classes. The tall building at 39 Rue Descartes, where Hemingway wrote for a while and the poet Paul Verlaine died, now houses a tacky bistro with a F69 menu.

However, on a weekday morning when the streets are quiet, there is nothing better than mooching round Hem's patch (as his mates called him), and following routes like the one quoted above which led him alternately to wine and words. The 5th was also home at that time to George Orwell, James Joyce and Jean Rhys. In the cafés a short walk away, like the Closerie des Lilas[1] and the Select[2] at Monparnasse, the ever-changing cast expanded to include Ezra Pound, F. Scott Fitzgerald and Ford Madox Ford. Many were refugees from prohibition in America.

Although Hemingway wrote in Rue Descartes, he lived with his first wife at 74 Rue du Cardinal Lemoine 'in a two-room flat that had no hot water and no inside toilet facilities except an antiseptic container, not uncomfortable to anyone who was used to a Michigan outhouse.' A fine view and a good mattress on the floor completed the attributes. Money was short, particularly when it came to buying food, and Hemingway recommended the aesthetic experience of seeing Cézanne's paintings on an empty stomach. Puzzlingly, he never seemed short of cash for drink, or betting on the races, and it is perhaps not surprising that he later broke up with his exasperated wife later.

None of the writers was bothered by lack of comfort. In 1928, Orwell moved in down the road, off the Rue du Mouffetard market, at 6 Rue du Pot-de-Fer. He says the concierge in the equally grotty hotel opposite once came out to berate one of her residents for squashing bed bugs on the wallpaper: 'Why can't you throw them out of the window like everyone else?'

There are two ways of discovering Hemingway country. The first, and easiest, is to join Paris Walking Tours[3] for their two-hour walk round the area. The guide, Oriel Caine, includes the other landmarks on the hill Sainte Geneviève like the Panthéon and the church of St Etienne, and quotes from the various authors in the area. The walk is erudite, amusing and thoroughly recommended, for some walking tour companies can be simplistic and less than accurate. For the more independent, a copy of *Paris – A Literary Companion*[4] will take you to the essential sites. It includes maps and quotes from the appropriate works of many different authors which can be read on the doorstep or in the café in question.

The Hemingway addict must of course carry a copy of the novel *The Sun Also Rises* and *A Moveable Feast*, his non-fiction memoir of Paris. It is not one of Hemingway's greatest works, but it will tide you across on the Eurostar, bringing on hunger of both the physical and intellectual sort. As he notes: 'Paris was always worth it and you received return for whatever you brought to it. But this is how Paris was in the early days when we were very poor and very happy.'

1   CLOSERIE DES LILAS, 171 Boulevard du Montparnasse, 6th,
        M Vavin, 01 40 51 34 50.
2   THE SELECT, 99 Boulevard du Montparnasse, 6th, M Vavin,
        01 42 22 65 27.
3   PARIS WALKING TOURS, Hemingway's Paris, Fr60,
        01 48 09 21 40.
4   *Paris – A Literary Companion* by Ian Littlewood, John Murray, £11.99.

"I wish to draw your attention to Ernest Hemingway's only feminist moment, which occurred one morning in the 1920s, when he stayed home instead of writing in the Closerie des Lilas. Irritated by a café critic who kept telling him his work was 'too stark', Hem, holed up in the Rue du Cardinal Lemoine. 'So the next morning I woke early, boiled the rubber nipples and the bottles, made the formula, finished the bottling, gave Mr Bumby a bottle and worked on the dining-room table before anyone but he, F. Puss the cat and I were awake.' Sadly, these are the only mentions of Mr Bumby and F. Puss in the Nobel-prizewinner's *oeuvre*, since Hem soon came to favour bullfighting over bottle-feeding.

BIKE AND ROLLERBLADE

City on wheels

When the Paris police got rollerblades, and formed eight-man mobile squads 'to fight crime among pedestrians' and do one-legged wheelies, you knew that in-line skating was no longer the province of teenagers. The great democratization of rollerblading took place during the annual winter strikes of the Métro and buses, leaving grown-up commuters in search of non-unionized wheels. Bikes and rollerblades sold out, and citizens of this largely flat city found they got to work faster, and stuck with self-propelled transport.

The visitor need not buy a bike or skates to go native in order to pose on the concrete expanses at La Défense, Palais Royal or Trocadéro, or to benefit from the special Sunday traffic-free lanes along the quais of the Seine. All equipment can be rented from Fr25 an hour to Fr60-110 a day at skate and bike shops around the city. The conveniently central Bike 'n' Roller has also had the splendid idea of giving city tours on rollerblade; a bilingual American ex-ice-skating champion (naturally) takes you speedily round major sites in the 5th and 6th *arrondissement*.

There was a great fuss made a couple of years ago

when Paris instituted its first bicycle lanes, years behind every other European city. The land of the Tour de France was in fact filled with drivers who found it difficult to grasp the idea that cyclists should be given priority rather than used as targets. The plastic bollards marking the cycle tracks were regularly mown down, and delivery vans did their best to park for as long as possible in the lanes and dump rotten market fruit in them. Not always verbal violence ensued. Ironically, if you were caught pedalling outside the lanes, you could be fined Fr230. Slightly more respect is shown to cyclists now, but there are only a few bike lanes each running north-south or east-west. Thus non-commuter cyclists, like bladers, prefer quiet Sundays when the roads are empty and the Seine quais are closed from 10am to 5pm to motor traffic, making them a bike and bladers' paradise.

Whereas in New York or even central London, urban cyclists feel it necessary to put on tourniquet-style shorts and fluorescent items, here you can be perfectly BCBG (*bon chic bon genre*) on yer bike. Short skirts, highish heels and the thinnest possible tights are acceptable for women, and men still favour suits and donnish cycle clips, with bungees to hold their leather briefcases on the racks. You can take bikes free on Ile de France trains except during the rush hour, but spots like Versailles and the Bois du Boulogne rent out their own, as well as bikes for children and baby seats.

Rollerblading has its own culture here like anywhere else. You can spot *les dweebs* – newcomers – here because they still wear knee pads and come to grief regularly on the Paris cobbles, which ruin a smooth ride for anyone. At 10 o'clock every Friday evening, skateposses – if that is the collective noun – of thousands of *les rollers* gather and race through the city. Usually they assemble at Trocadéro for the Right Bank cruise and Place d'Italie for the Left Bank and the quais by streetlight. The latest information can be gleaned from any skate shop. Most hire shops also offer lessons and rent out protective equipment to initiates.

> BIKE 'N' ROLLER, 6 Rue St-Julien-le-Pauvre, 5th, M St Michel, 01 44 07 35 89,: cellar near Notre Dame is one of the most convenient, but expensive, with mountain bikes from around Fr100 a day and rollerblades from Fr75 plus deposit. There are lessons available on certain days, and the Paris on Blades roller tour. Call for details.
>
> ROLLER STATION has two branches, 140 Avenue du Maine, 14th, M Gaîté, 01 43 20 82 27 (closed Mon) and 107 Boulevard Beaumarchais, 3rd, M St Sebastien-Froissart, 01 42 78 33 00, Fr60 a day, Fr100 a weekend, plus Fr1,000 deposit.
>
> ROLLERMANIA, 131 Rue de la Santé, 13th, 01 45 80 92 71, is an association which provides information on shops and events. It is not open to the public, but they will answer queries by phone and mail.
>
> BIKE RENTALS from: PARIS-VELO, 2 Rue Fer-à-Moulin, 5th, M Censier-Daubenton, 01 43 37 59 22 and MAISON DE VELO, 11 Rue Fénélon, 10th, M Gare du Nord, 01 42 81 24 72.
>
> Reading: *Faire du vélo à Paris*, Parigramme, Fr35.

" It costs £200 million a year to clean the streets of the city, £10,000 of which is dedicated to canine sanitation: this is a country which will never descend to the pooper-scooper. Instead, there is a fleet of 75 *motocrottes* – motorbikes with vacuums. But in the forward-thinking 13th *arrondissement*, signs have begun to appear featuring a Lassie-like cartoon: dogposts.

To a dog, the 'canine rest areas' provide all the tactile pleasures of a lamppost, but are surrounded by a small sandpit, emptied five times a day. Unfortunately,

when the scheme was piloted, dogs gave it a wide
berth. It was at this point the 'canine counsellors' were
brought in to buttonhole the unwary. 'We estimate
that only 20 per cent of the dogs' masters are ill-
disciplined,' say the counsellors. 'Our mission is to
inform and convince. Fines of up to £100 will be
waived if the perpetrator agrees to attend a lecture
on the exorbitant costs.' Collection of the detritus is
somewhat expensive – at Fr 37 a kilo, it compares with
the best asparagus.

SHOPPING SECRETS

HIGH TAT

Bargains in the Goutte d'Or

After a couple of days shopping in Paris you get all Faubourg'd out. You want prices with fewer zeros on the end; you want the sleaze and exotica of the cut-price Goutte d'Or.

Just one Métro stop past the Gare du Nord, there is a warren of stores and markets surpassing Woolworths, the five 'n' dime, and even the nasty end of Oxford Street – probably the only place in this extortionate city where, were it that time of year, you could complete your entire Christmas shopping for under 20 quid.

Although the jewel of Boulevard Rochechouart is the Tati[1] department store, its pink-checked plastic bags the very symbol of economy and tatty chic, the area is also full of curious Algerian and African shops, selling everything from outlandish dress materials to gilt-etched glasses for mint tea. A few steps up the hill towards the Sacré Coeur are Paris's best discount fabric shops in the Marché St Pierre.

As you emerge into the bustle and madness above the Métro Barbès-Rochechouart, men compete to hand you slips of paper: 'Professor Kaba, celebrated medium and seer,' said one. 'Helps those who have need of high magic. Love – Money – Health. Protection assured against enemies, exams, business difficulties. Hundred per cent success in births. Receives visitors seven days a week, 9am to 9pm.' If you need a witch doctor, *un marabout*, this is the place to come.

But before you can even contemplate putting a curse on someone, the crowd's momentum whisks you into Tati, with boxes of toy tractors and Barbies piled high, acres of women's clothes for under a tenner. Look, however, and you shall find. Among the rubbish there are turquoise and yellow glazed Moroccan vases and plates for F50. Chanel-style chain belts in silver or tortoiseshell for F39, and black plastic skirts and coats at silly prices, to be worn for one silly season. With a sharp eye, coupled with sharp elbows for moving through the crowd, you may even reach the cash desk.

This is not a place to come overdressed, or with a fancy handbag – a little care is required to avoid becoming an obvious target for pickpockets. For clothes, many fashionable students swear by Guerrisold[2] on Boulevard Barbès, with new and secondhand items costing from F50. Magazine stylists come here for little 1970s-inspired numbers.

This whole area is known as the 'Goutte d'Or', the drop of gold, after the hill which produced fine wine in the Middle Ages. Now the Rue de la Goutte d'Or still trades in gold and silver fabrics, richly embroidered velvets, and wedding shoes crunchy with sequins and glitter. The next street up, Rue des Poissonières, is full of African cloths and spices, and turbanned salesmen dressed more for the bazaar than the Paris streets. There are shops selling Moroccan teapots, sets of six tea glasses, and 'African Pride Castor and Mink Oil' hair pomade.

Five minutes up the hill towards the Sacré Coeur, there is the Place St Pierre, cloth central. Every fabric found in the centre of Paris with a F500 a metre price tag is here for F50, looking little different. In a scattering of department stores, all those grand woven upholstery fabrics found on Louis-something chairs abound, as are *toiles de jouy* – cream material printed with red or blue bucolic scenes.

The Marché St Pierre is where the clever Parisian clothes her home from stores like Moline[3] and Dreyfus[4], where bales of material pour from the doors into the street. Generally, the cheap stuff at F20 a metre is on the ground floor, but bargains of wonderful quality are upstairs for more. Dreyfus has Provençal fabrics, with olive and lemon patterns on blue or yellow backgrounds for F29, and Moline, slightly more upmarket versions for F49. The stores also stock all the necessary buttons, linings and ribbons.

For sustenance after the shopping scrum, there is the Halle St Pierre, gutted and modernized to include a tea salon with the newspapers and a folk art museum. Its huge arched windows look up over the park towards the Sacré Coeur.

1   TATI, 4 Boulevard Rochechouart, 18th, M Barbès-Rochechouart, 01 42 55 13 09.
2   GUERRISOLD, 9 and 21 Boulevard Barbès, 9th, 01 42 52 39 24.
3   MOLINE, 1 Place St Pierre, 18th, 01 46 06 14 66.
4   DREYFUS, 2 Rue Charles Nodier, 18th, 01 46 06 92 25.

      Tati still has something of the souk about it. It was
opened in 1948 by Jules Ouaki after being demobbed
from the Free French, and he named the corner shop
after his grandmother. Now his son Fabien runs 36
stores and is opening another in New York, where Tati
is already famous from a series of pink-and-white
checked Julian Schnabel paintings.

      Obviously, in Britain you will be unable to obtain
Tati magazine, which gives useful tips on leading life
according to the Tati philosophy, disputing parking
tickets, finding a map of radar speed traps and
economizing on telephone bills. Soon, however, the
www.tati.fr. website will be on line.

      Recognizing at last that Tati was terminally hip, the
Museum of Decorative Arts at the Louvre dedicated
an exhibition to the phenomenon, and invited 50
photographers and celebrities to create their own
image of Tati. Catherine Deneuve, Jean-Loup Sieff,
Nan Goldin, Britain's Martin Parr and our favourite
Eurotrash philosopher, Bernard-Henri Lévy, all
provided works. The stairs leading to the exhibition
were peopled by 100 mannequins, naked but for a
bikini or an apron made from a Tati bag.

      Big Girls' Blouses are unavailable in Paris, as are any
clothes in sizes much beyond 38 (a weeny size 10).
Post-pregnancy, I cruised into Agnès b to celebrate the
return of a body verging on normal. Minutes later, a
supercilious assistant found me on the floor of the
changing room, permanently trapped in a pair of
hipsters. I crawled weeping from the shop.

      Over a leaf of the latest lettuce with my friend Jane

(a pleasant size 14), I asked her why she was not naked. 'That's easy,' she said. 'All designer shops secretly have big clothes, but they only put the small ones on the rack to impress. So you go in the back and whisper: "Excuse me, have you any embarrassingly gross sizes?" The assistant looks at you pityingly and then sneaks the fat clothes under the counter without anyone seeing the labels.'

THE
DROUOT

From andouillette to auction

Here is a recipe for what may either be an economical or expensive midday, depending on self control: lunch at Chartier[1], the cheapest and grandest brasserie in town, followed by the 2pm daily auction at Le Drouot, the bizarre salerooms two blocks away. It is ideal for travellers disaffected by too many museums, shops and Americans. Off the tourist beat, you can lunch cannily at one of Paris's finest art nouveau bistros and, if you have any knowledge of antiques, paintings and French numbers, bid cannily too.

The atmosphere and sense of drama is similar in both establishments, embodying the finest Gallic traditions, and one day soon will probably be extinct, the brasserie wiped out by Le McDo — cheap burgers garishly advertised down the street — and the disorganized auction rooms destroyed by multinational Christie's and Sotheby's.

Just before 1pm, you enter Chartier through a cobbled courtyard off the Rue du Faubourg Montmartre, and are swung back into the nineteenth century through the revolving doors. There's no need to book. The place serves hundreds, and they just pack complete strangers on to giant tables. This being Paris, there's no need to converse, but you can eavesdrop.

Long lines of tables, with cloths covered in paper on which the waiter scribbles your order and bill, stretch beneath art nouveau globe lights, and brass coat hooks. The floor is crazily tiled, and a Greek statue observes the hubbub from a niche in the wall. In 1996, Chartier celebrated its 100th anniversary as a *bouillon*, a working-class bistro. By quickly serving vast numbers with good, bulk-bought meat, Chartier became the sophisticated McDo of its day.

Chartier prints a menu every day, and it is probably the only one in Paris with some courses still in single figures. I've had *salade de tomate* and *merlan* (whiting) *braisé au muscadet*, a plateful of bread and a carafe of water for Fr49 including tip.

I shared a table that day with a sixtyish woman in Dame Edna glasses and an original orange and green polyester dress, now being much copied by Prada. What I like about the French is that they have no hesitation about interfering when food is at stake. 'Not much to eat on that, is there?' said the woman, peering over her spectacles, ready to poke my fish with her knife.

'Can you actually taste the muscadet?' she checked.

I nodded.

'You're sure? Then I'll change my order. Waiter!'

When her beady-eyed whiting arrived, she complained to the waiter that it was smaller than mine. Then she consumed pills from two dark bottles, and a carafe of throat-rasping red wine, the masochist's choice at Fr9. She confessed she had been eating regularly at Chartier for 18 years and generally the food was pretty good, although she did not recommend the *andouillette grillée 5AAAAA* – which translates as awful offal sausage.

A five-minute walk away at L'Hôtel Drouot[2] on Rue Drouot, there was much anticipation and scrabbling for seats as the two o'clock auctions began. With 16 rooms running at once, I was torn between wine auctions selling off fine Château Margaux, household auctions selling Persian rugs and leather riding boots, and a sculpture sale which included Man Ray's *A Present* – a smoothing iron with rusty nails driven in the front (estimate Fr4,000).

The auction style has not changed much since the state-run L'Hôtel Drouot opened in 1556. Sometimes there are glossy catalogues to consult, but often there is just a dog-eared typed list. There is a nice class divide depending on the contents of each auction. In the house salerooms, men with dandruff and leather jackets clash over crates of disused tape recorders, and often leave armed with a Hoover. In the art sales, there is merely the clash of fine aftershaves, and ladies with nothing better to do than sit with poodles on their knees, bidding politely.

Although there are previews daily at 11am, the delight of the Drouot is its unexpectedness. It's been known to auction Tintin memorabilia and the world's most expensive potatoes at £180 per pound. It publishes a monthly magazine which lists forthcoming sales, and there are bank dispensers in the halls outside the salerooms, because the auctioneers – unless they know and love you – prefer their cash hard.

1   CHARTIER, 7 Rue du Faubourg Montmartre, 9th, M Rue
      Montmartre, 01 47 70 86 29.
2   DROUOT AUCTION ROOMS, 9 Rue Drouot, 9th, 01 48 00 20 20.

"One day I fell upon a sale of what seemed to be the personal effects of an august and ancient madame. The auctioneer, a grey-haired man with a spray-on tan, had his male minions parade in the mink stoles pulled from crates, puff old perfume bottles into the air and wave hats to his ironic *Ooh là làs*. Madame would have been scandalized. The objects of her life provided a mini-biography for the crowd: Gothic armoires, size 14 dresses, Chinese rugs, a doll's leather coat. The book dealers were jockeying round crates of her first editions when the auctioneer's assistant waved a book for all to see. '*Le Marquis de Sade!*' he hooted. Madame would have been somewhat embarrassed.

FABRIC FOR KINGS

Marie Antoinette's summer curtains

Down a dusty street behind the Opéra is a shop which looks as if it has been closed for 20 years. The window has a grubby brown curtain and the decrepit sign for 'Georges le Manach: Textiles' does not inspire confidence.

We push the handle. The room is empty except for a rotund man who points us upstairs, past a sheet of exquisite red-and-gold cloth so heavy that it might fall from its wooden stand. On the walls are framed pieces of material with the words: 'English imitation: To Copy is to Steal'. We have entered the secret, almost masonic, world of the grand Parisian fabric shop.[1]

Upstairs they really do make cloth of gold, and silk and velvet. The walls are draped with original patterns from the reigns of Louis III to Napoleon III. A metre of their finest cloth trailed with velvet flowers on silk and hand embroidered costs £2,760.

Of course, ordinary mortals may not enter the exclusive premises of le Manach, where they normally deal with wholesalers, professionals and customers such as John Paul Getty – which is why I have recruited as chaperon

Joanna Bates,[2] an English interior designer who lives and works in Paris.

Trained at Colefax and Fowler in England, Ms Bates has discovered the curious literary and political under-pinnings of French fabric. As Louis followed Louis, curtains and hangings reflected each king's conquests and desires. Louis XV banned Indian cloth and insisted (*plus ça change*) that the French should buy expensive French products. Thus pseudo-Indian cloth was created by little men in St. Malo. Ms Bates points out a bold design called Victor Hugo, a pattern commissioned by the great nineteenth century writer for his salon.

Historical accuracy matters here, which is partly why such showrooms survive. 'French traditional interior design is very purist,' says Ms Bates. 'A Louis XV drawing-room must have Louis XV material on every chair whereas the British and Americans here are happy to mix ancient and modern.'

The grand French colonial tradition does not go unrecorded. From the early 1900s there are velvety safari fabrics, leopard and zebra, modelled exactly on the animal skins. 'Very modern,' says Ms Bates. At nearly £1,000 a metre, it is probably cheaper to shoot your own.

The most amusing fabric, created during the Revolution of 1789, is red, white and blue and now available at a suitably patriotic price of £32 a metre. It is covered with fat-armed peasants holding scrolls of the Declaration of the Rights of Man.

From the peasants we move across to the aristocracy, into the nearby wood-panelled showroom of Tassinari and Chatel, established in 1680. The light curtains at the windows, of green oak leaves and acorns, are from Marie

Antoinette's summer drawing-room. We gaze at the pale
grey, blue and yellow silk from the Versailles billiard room
at £450 a metre

The company has recently replaced the entire
hangings of Louis XV's bedroom at the palace. We turn
the cerise-and-green sample over to see, in the careful
embroidery, real gold thread as thick as wire.

Where once the royal palaces were big customers,
now political palaces have taken their place. Trade is not
quite what it was, but the Elysée, home to President Chirac,
and the Hôtel Matignon, home to the Prime Minister, Alain
Juppé, are regular customers at Braquenie near the Marais.
There, a terrifying Madame in black gives the tour. The
problem with modern clients, she complains, is that they
are so conservative compared with the revolutionaries and
royalty of the past.

'All they want is beige and salmon, beige and
salmon. And they won't mix patterns.' She shrugs in
despair.

1   Dozens of traditional textile shops are open to the public in the
        triangle of the Place de Furstenberg, Rue Jacob and Rue Bonaparte
        on the Left Bank.
2   JOANNA BATES INTERIOR DESIGN, 7 Rue des Canettes, Paris
        6th, 01 46 33 00 31.
Also: MARCHE ST PIERRE fabric market, Place St Pierre, 18th, M Anvers.

❝I always prefer, when settling in a new city, to live
    as close as possible to a good taxidermist. In London
    we were fortunate enough to live above a grocer's
    shop opposite Get Stuffed, a jewel of the Essex Road.
    Here in Paris we are just yards from the taxidermist

Deyrolle, which has been stuffing tigers and Egyptian dung beetles since 1831 (Deyrolle, 47 Rue du Bac, 01 42 22 30 07). Very little – including the shop's décor – has changed since those days when French explorers returned from the Dark Continent with extraordinary specimens and complicated skin disorders.

A grand wooden staircase leads past displays of giant ants to the zoo-of-the-dead. There are no glass cases, so a lioness, a zebra and a horse strut the ravaged parquet beneath the once-turquoise paint. Wooden drawers stretch high, filled with butterflies. Three human skulls smile in a row. In dark corners, wolves and polar bears roam.

My sons and I have become regulars at Deyrolle on rainy afternoons, and the staff seem to object neither to the mooing and growling noises we make, nor to the fact we never buy anything. We are now friends with Arnaud, a taxidermist with five years' experience.

He laments that trade in larger items such as sharks and jaguars is falling – 'but we're big on rentals for parties and films' – and that much of his work is mounting hunting trophies.

The great art of taxidermy is being frittered away on domestic pets called Fifi and Minouche. On one visit, we paused before a sickly miniature King Charles Spaniel. 'How much would stuffing that cost?' I asked. 'About Fr3,700 for that, going up to Fr9,000 for a large dog,' said Arnaud. Meanwhile, my youngest son was patting a poodle, quite unaware that it had passed away.

Did Arnaud witness cases of post-taxidermy trauma, when owners refused to take their ex-pets home?

'Definitely,' he said. 'Where do you think we got all these?' I had a final question: was there a stage when a dead cat, say, might be too ripe for stuffing? 'No, no. Stick it in your freezer and it'll keep six or seven months, no problem.'

DESIGNERS
SECONDHAND

Cheap bon chic bon genre

The inexplicable thing about elegant Parisian women is: where do they get the money? A certain percentage work in fashion, or have a rich lover, but what of the rest? Be assured, they earn little more than Britons do, yet they look twice the woman. As it turns out, any Parisian label-junkie, worth her Hermès, heads to the *dépôts-ventes*, the shops which specialize in pristine secondhand couture. She just wouldn't tell *you* that.

Many of these shops are in the chi-chi 16th *arrondissement*, where the richest women in Paris tend to live and shed their clothes four times a year with the social seasons. So there are Chanel suits not long off the catwalk, Hermès scarves, Yves Saint-Laurent, Valentino, Alaïa, Ungaro, Kenzo, and even the more radical Moschino and Vivienne Westwood, all at half or a third of the original price.

Remember, however, that the original price was gargantuan. Banish thoughts of Oxfam and Camden and their bargains from your head, and reach deep for your credit cards. The *dépôts-ventes* are only for the serious shopper obsessed with big-name designers, and looking for rather grand clothes. The casual tourist with a few hours to spare should not attempt that which takes a Frenchwoman with a well-honed eye a whole afternoon.

The largest secondhand shop in Paris is Réciproque[1] on Rue de la Pompe. If you take the Métro to La Muette, at the start of the street and walk north, you will pass L'Occaserie,[2] a smaller and cheaper version. The first L'Occaserie at number 19 specializes in designer baby and maternity clothes. It is fine for party dresses, blazers and those Austrian-style woollen jackets with contrasting piping, but children's clothes are not cheap, and often rather over-washed by the time they reach the shop.

A block up is L'Occaserie for women, its window filled with Chanel chain-logo belts at £235, and endless earrings with intertwined Cs. Inside, there is a stiff proprietress who watches customers suspiciously, and one suspects she drives a hard bargain with the ladies of the 16th who offer their wardrobes. These savings are not, of course, passed on to the customer, but careful research in the racks unearths a Guy Laroche short black evening dress with *diamanté* buttons for just over £100, and an Yves Saint-Laurent 'le smoking' suit with a skirt for £300. There are also Montana and Lacroix jackets for £130, an Isaac Mizrahi green and white patent bag for £60, and the eternal Hermès scarf for £80.

Further up the street is Réciproque, secondhand Mecca for many Parisians. There are five different specialist shops, for women's daywear, eveningwear, menswear, accessories and coats on both sides of the street. The accessories shop has an entire back room dedicated to handbags, including a Hermès antique in crocodile for a stunning £3,500. For £50 or so, however, you can come away with a chic bag with a blatant designer label.

As I lurked, a grandly dressed lady in her sixties bought some Chanel earrings. 'Have you a box? It's a present,' she said unashamed. The saleswoman unlocked a cupboard full of new-looking little boxes with various designers' logos, and the present was passed off as brand new.

Across in the suit and eveningwear department, the clothes are neatly ranked by designer, colour and size – a great deal in size 10. A short pink tweed Chanel suit was over £1,000, but would be twice that new. Many of the buttons had been snipped off the Chanels on the racks, and presumably sewn convincingly on some cheaper garment at home. The ladies of the 16th may be rich, but they are not extravagant.

Over in the 2nd *arrondissement*, in a pretty arcade near the Bourse, there is La Marelle.[3] The labels here are not so grand, but the clothes are more youthful – Joseph, Kenzo, Agnès b – and the bargains are better. A brown velvet Joseph redingote in perfect condition was under £100, and there are also smart children's dresses and shoes.

1   RECIPROQUE, 92, 93, 95, 101 and 123 Rue de la Pompe, 16th, M Rue
       de la Pompe, 01 47 04 30 28.
2   L'OCCASERIE, 19 and 30 Rue de la Pompe, 16th, M La Muette,
       01 45 03 16 56.
3   LA MARELLE, 23 Galerie Vivienne, 2nd, M Bourse, 01 42 60 08 19.

Reading: *Comment devenir une vrai parisienne*, Parigramme, Fr35. *Le Guide Paris Combines*, M.A. Editions at Paris bookshops has a comprehensive list of *dépôts-ventes*.

❝Semiologists – who tend to be men – used to say the symbols of France were the bug-eyed Citroën DS, the baguette and Bardot. Nowadays Bardot is a barking cat lady who flirts with the National Front; the baguette has been replaced by Pain Poilâne in modish sandwiches; and the Citroën has given way to the Renault Twingo. There is a move to anoint the demi-Badoit, the half bottle of fizzy salt water on every restaurant table, as the new icon of the nation. But I wish to put forward what should be a more durable symbol: A Good Handbag.

You can wear the nastiest polyester from the Monoprix chainstore, but if you carry the right bag – brand-name leather – you will be respected in your native land. You can always spot tourists in the Métro: they try to dress smartly like Parisians, but their grubby little backpacks give them away.

The Good Handbag is no frivolous matter. A famous human rights lawyer is never seen without her Lacroix clutch. Bernadette Chirac, the president's wife, was caricatured on *Les Guignols* television puppet show kissing her favourite Chanel bag.

Recently, Marie Darrieussecq, a young novelist much fêted in intellectual journals confessed: 'I have a red Lancel, a backpack, which I bought with the first advance for *Truismes* [plot: woman metamorphoses into sow]. It was a long-held dream: I never thought that one day I'd be able to buy a Lancel. It cost me £150.'

Darrieussecq also reveals she has a little leather 'lady's bag' and a yellow number from Paquetage for carrying piles of literature. 'I love bags,' says the respected writer. 'But in general I consider myself a

serious person. Sometimes I ask myself how much
superficiality one's existence requires.'

❝I was in a changing room in the Galeries Lafayette,
trying on a striped T shirt. I put a jacket on top and
stared uneasily. 'No, you shouldn't buy that. Doesn't
suit you,' advised a kindly Parisian co-customer in a
size eight. 'The jacket waist is far too high and the
colour's unflattering.'

'Thanks,' I said, 'It's my own jacket, I've had it for a
year.'

Attempting to regain confidence in my taste and
mysteriously low-slung waist, I then tried on some
trousers in Allison on the Rue du Bac. 'You'll take
them,' ordered the saleswoman. 'Nah, they're cut a bid
oddly,' I said. She rose up. 'There's nothing odd about
these trousers. The problem is your shoes. You can't
possibly wear trousers of this quality with shoes like
that,' she spat.

Am confining myself to mail-order shopping from
the Sackcloth and Ashes catalogue and making no
observations whatsoever about Parisian manners.

FLEA
MARKETS

Coping with Clignancourt

Rancid chip fat hits the nostrils and cross-pongs with hot sugared nuts. Cloying men keep trying to force leather jackets or baseball caps into your arms. Three-card trick players rip off Japanese tourists. Then you feel someone pull the zip on your bag. You want to go home.

The problem with Paris's fleamarkets is that they can seem a little fleabitten and tacky unless you know exactly where to go, and when. The visitor must run the gauntlet of modern tat to reach the ancient centre. Military precision and the ability to ignore the inessential are required for any success. Bargains are not a matter of chance, but of effort.

There are three major fleamarkets, or *puces*, at Saint-Ouen (Clignancourt), Vanves and Montreuil. Clignancourt is the largest. Montreuil[1] is exotic and scruffy, good for secondhand clothes and junk, but not much else. Still, there is a stall selling secondhand theatre costumes, and I know people who have picked up Agnès b popper tops for Fr20 here, and 1950s dresses for F100. The stalls which have sorted out clothing, dry-cleaned it and stuck it on hangers mean you spend little time finding the object of desire, but much more money. If you're willing to rummage through boxes on grubby stalls, however, Hermès and Chanel may eventually cross your palm.

More worth the Métro schlepp is the market along Avenue Georges-Lafenestre, two minutes' walk from Porte de Vanves Métro. Zoom past the initial stalls selling goods that fell-off-a-lorry, and you can haggle for small household items, easy to carry home and without doubt weird.

A fruitbowl of old billiard balls with fading paint looks promising. For Fr10 there are sepia photographs from family albums – Victorian ladies playing stiff croquet on the beach. Someone picked up the oldest existing daguerrotype here recently for a cool £60 – it's just a question of having a sharp eye. The silver-plated cutlery is old hotel stuff, but grand silver ladles go for a fair £12. Perhaps, a mile down the road, there is a hot chocolate stall for rejuvenation, before the market takes a turn into Rue Marc-Sagnier where the clothes begin.

Vanves[2] is simple, cheap and not too time-consuming, but the real sights are to be found at Clignancourt[3], the world's biggest fleamarket. Paris's *puces* all ended up around the *péripherique* ringroad after the 1832 cholera epidemic brought on an obsession with cleanliness and the rag and bone trade was forced beyond the city walls.

Clignancourt has gone up in the world since those days. A Napoleon III chair will set you back a good thousand pounds, depending on condition. The few rag and junk merchants lurk at the furthest reaches of alleys.

There are at least 16 different markets, some easy to miss. The best method is: sprint through the modern stalls before and after the *péripherique*. Make for the Rue des Rosiers, where the information office sometimes has maps, and nip in and out of markets on either side, always returning to the main drag.

First you pass the large Marché Vernaison, full of old and new furniture, porcelain dolls, unmatched china, all displayed in small shacks. There are fabulous old poster shops, and stalls selling crisp old linen and *toiles de jouy*, those red and blue prints of country scenes on white. In the Vernaison there is also the Chez Louisette restaurant, an ancient, rather cheesy favourite. In general, you want to stick to coffee near the markets, and eat elsewhere afterwards.

Coming up next are the Malassis and Dauphine markets – 200 antique dealers in a modern building with a café, and the all-important cashpoint, because most dealers prefer francs over French cheques, and offering credit cards results in refusal or an instant price hike.

Opposite is the Marché Biron, a grand row of little antique shops, each like a room from a different era. They are big on Louisomething, indeed Louisanything, and everything is so over-restored it looks, or perhaps is, rather new. The prices are high but the variety is huge, increasing your bargaining power. The Biron's Allée 2, the back corridor, is generally cheaper and more fascinating. Useful tip: the public loos are here too.

Next is the Marché Serpette, the interior decorators' haunt, with great art nouveau and deco, chandeliers and fine furniture. This has become an expensive mecca for leather armchairs too. Right next door is the Marché Paul-Bert, open air with scroggy antiques and bargains. Down the Rue Paul-Bert the visit ends with the super-junky Marché Jules Valles.

The best day for Clignancourt is actually Friday,

when the market is only supposed to be open to dealers, and new stuff appears. But on Sunday afternoon the place is crowded and atmospheric. Many stallholders will have brought a plastic-flowered tablecloth and set up for lunch near their stalls with a baguette, good Camembert and red wine. Prices drop as the afternoon wears on.

The stallholders tend to buy their wares out of town, or at specialized *brocantes* advertized in the monthly dealer's magazine, *Aladin*, available from newsagents. On the first Saturday of each month, the Salvation Army holds a giant household sale in its shop L'Arche de l'Espoir[4] in the 13th *arrondissement*. Plates go for Fr2, tables from Fr80, and a 1796 chair for Fr4,800, but ring first for details.

1   MARCHÉ DE LA PORTE DE MONTREUIL, M Porte de Montreuil. Sat, Sun, Mon
2   MARCHÉ DE LA PORTE DE VANVES, M Porte de Vanves. Sat, Sun
3   MARCHÉ DE ST OUEN, Fri (dealers), M Clignancourt. Sat, Sun, Mon
4   L'ARCHE DE L'ESPOIR shop, 12, Rue Cantagrel, 13th, M Porte d'Ivry, call 01 53 61 82 45. Hours vary.
Reading: *Guide to Markets in Paris* by Nadia Pret, Syros Alternatives.

“ We're rooting round the furniture stalls of Clignancourt, once a fleamarket, now a fleece market. There is an uprising among the small people demanding sustenance. No McDonald's here. Hysteria rises. Then we hear a Hammond organ. A gin-throaty ballad and the smell of greasy chips come up the alleyway. It is Chez Louisette, a *gargote* (which translates as grotty wee restaurant) deep in the Marché Vernaison. Inside the fug of the home-built wooden cabin, there are pillars festooned with

man-size Wild Turkey bottles, year-round Christmas
decorations and tables with yellow paper tablecloths.
The floor is sticky, like Velcro beneath your feet.
It's our kind of place.

At the organ there's a fat grey-permed corpse with
bottle glasses. Only her finger moves on the auto-
drum button. We work out she's alive when she stops
to smoke. An Andean guitarist leaps on to the tiny
stage: long hair, white flares, two medallions, platform
trainers – full glam-rock revival (except he doesn't
know about the revival). His mike stand is counter-
balanced by a big Christmas-tree bauble.

My younger son is enraptured. For the first time
in his one-and-a-half years he sits still in a grown-up
chair for almost an hour occasionally clapping and
swaying. A woman in satin sings '*La Vie en Rose*' (natch).
Old ladies take it seriously and order Piña Coladas,
while French yuppies snigger into their Barbours.

Some detumescent grey things arrive on a plate.
They're green beans. Something's bleeding beside
them. The steak. I think that probably the sanest cows
just look mad, and eat up. The kids stick sensibly to
chips. What's the husband got? 'A sort of veal in a
cream sauce wrapped round cheese with crispy, um, is
that mushrooms and what are these?' he says. We drink
deep of the tonsil-torquing wine. My elder son is on
the cusp of ironic knowledge and sits suspiciously
eating his chips, not sure what the in-joke is. 'It's not
Christmas, is it?' he asks. No. Time for a new word.
Kitsch.

BOOKS AND BOUQUINISTERS

English and French lit

The dignified Galignani[1] opposite the Tuileries was the first English bookshop to open in Paris in 1802. Later, Gertrude Stein used to walk by the windows and thrill to the sight of her own books in her own bizarre language. Because Paris attracts so many ex-pat writers and long-term tourists, the Anglo-Saxon bookshops continue to multiply. They are part of legend. The famous Shakespeare and Co[2] isn't what it was in the days when Sylvia Beach gave Hemingway loans for his bar bill. The shop is no longer on Beach's original site, but some of the ethos remains; hand-written notices, general chaos, and new and used books in English.

Most of the guides and reference books mentioned in this book are to be found at Brentanos or W.H. Smith in the city centre. Brentanos[3] is more American, has a good children's section in both languages, and a peculiarly large selection of quilting magazines, presumably for those who wish they were down home. W.H. Smith[4] is sizeable and open on Sundays. There's a great English and American magazine and newspaper section, where you can browse free for hours.

For the true French experience, you must turn to the

Fnac⁵ chain which stocks everything, or trawl the Left
Bank, which is littered with specialist bookshops and the
bouquinistes stalls along the Seine. La Hune, in St Germain,
is decadent enough to open until midnight.

1   GALIGNANI, 224 Rue de Rivoli, 1st, M Tuileries, 01 42 60 76 07.
2   SHAKESPEARE AND CO, 37 Rue de la Bucherie, 5th, M Maubert-
        Mutualité, 01 43 26 96 50.
3   BRENTANOS, 37 Avenue de l'Opéra, 2nd, M Opéra, 01 42 61 52 50.
4   W.H. SMITH, 248 Rue de Rivoli, 1st, M Concorde, 01 44 77 88 99.
5   FNAC, 74 Avenue des Champs-Elysées, 8th, M Franklin D. Roosevelt,
        01 53 53 64 64.
6   La Hune, 170 Boulevard St Germain, 6th, M St German,
        01 45 48 35 86.

MINI-
MUSEUMS

JACQUEMART-ANDRE
MUSEUM

Separate beds, shared art

When Mademoiselle Nélie Jacquemart, a spinster of some 40 years and no beauty, snared one of Paris's most eligible bachelors, society could talk of little else. The improbable match of Edouard André, a Protestant banker and art lover, and Mlle Jacquemart, a low-born Catholic portrait painter, was the scandal of summer 1881. In *hôtels particuliers* all along the up-and-coming Boulevard Haussmann, mothers bemoaned M. André's loss to their débutante daughters. What, they wondered, could Mlle Jacquemart offer that their fresh young girls could not? The answer was good taste – and an eye for a bargain Botticelli.

For Nélie and Edouard were united by a passion for art more than for each other. They slept in separate beds, produced no children, but together spawned the finest private art collection in Paris. They were, in some ways, the Saatchis or Gettys of their day, turning their magnificent mansion on Boulevard Haussmann into a live-in museum. They had Rembrandts in the library, Gainsboroughs in the smoking room, marble busts in the boudoir, Uccellos upstairs, and Fragonards everywhere else.

Each summer, the Andrés went to Italy to pick up

Canalettos and other souvenirs, and they were not above coming home with entire ceilings and fireplaces, or a 30-foot mural by Tiepolo, which hangs in the hall. Their relationship with dealers and auctioneers was cordial, since they had an annual art budget of between Fr223,000 and Fr514,000. Compare this to the Louvre itself, which had a state budget of Fr200,000 a year. The Andrés were buying not just for themselves but for *la patrimonie*, France's heritage. Indeed, before one important auction, the Louvre's curator wrote to Nélie saying: 'I am counting on you to compensate for our museum's lack of funds.'

The Andrés left their mansion to L'Institut de France, and part of it opened in 1913 as the Museum Jacquemart-André.[1] Rather like the Frick in New York or the Wallace Collection in London, it has the intimacy of a home, with the grandeur of great art.

By the early 1990s, the Jacquemart-André had become dull and dusty. The upper floors were out of bounds, the private chambers were offices, and the collection was badly displayed. It shut for four years, and fundraised wildly. The result, now open to the public, is a rebirth. For the first time we can see the private bedrooms of Nélie (double bed with yellow silk hangings) and André (single in dusty pink, panelled bath), and the antechamber in between, where they took breakfast together.

Visitors can ascend the gilt, wrought iron and marble double staircase to the upper floors, where the Andrés kept their Italian Museum, as a treat for dinner guests or art experts. There are marble fountains and Roman doorways set into the blue walls. There is Uccello's *St George and the Dragon*, and at least four radiant Madonnas with child, including the Botticelli which Nélie spotted, then unattributed.

There are also, sad to say, lots of visitors wandering around with those audio-tours clapped to their ears, so transfixed by the tape that they keep bumping into each other. Find a corner alone, however, and the lack (mostly) of red ropes and officialdom allows you to image the days of the strange liaison of Nélie and Edouard. Their parties, for instance, were to die for. When Edouard had the mansion built in 1875, he insisted that the reception rooms would have hydraulic walls which sank into the floor to create one enormous ballroom. *L'Illustration* magazine wrote that guests at an early ball included Countess Tolstoy, the Baronne de Rothschild, Countess Petrovska and one of the La Rochefoucaulds. 'The walls were smothered in a balmy canopy of violets and camellias, and lit by a thousand candles'. The evening was declared 'a dazzling enchantment . . . no more admirable setting can be imagined'.

1   HÔTEL JACQUEMART-ANDRÉ, 158 Boulevard Haussmann, 8th,
     M St Philippe-du-Roule, 01 42 89 04 91, 10am–6pm daily, Fr47.
     Café in the former dining-room open 11.30am-5.30pm.

❝There is a special circle of Hell reserved for museum guards, and Paris museum guards are right in the centre. There cannot be a species more formidable or intoxicated with their own power. I recently made the error of resting my notebook on a glass display case in the Delacroix museum to note down a letter to George Sand. Suddenly, a voice barked: '*S'il vous plaît, Madame!*', which is French for 'Get your grubby hands off there, ratface.'

I was lectured on the etiquette of not touching. The guard then tailed me for an hour. Days later, I peeked behind a curtain at the Victor Hugo musuem, to check his pleasant view across the Place des Vosges. I received a public warning and was moved on. This was nothing compared to the indignity inflicted on a flamboyant gay friend touring the porcelain-packed Cognacq-Jay museum in the Marais. A uniformed toad bustled up and said: 'Sir, there are delicate works here. Could you kindly refrain from using such expansive gestures in public?'

THE EDITH PIAF MUSEUM

Too camp to regret

Few know about the Edith Piaf Museum[1], and fewer still make the effort to visit it, thus it is the perfect antidote to a day queueing with five thousand others who want to be fed culture at the Louvre. But the Piaf fan must be dedicated, regretting nothing in his or her efforts to worship at the altar of the diva, for the museum is far off the beaten track in the 11th, near where Piaf grew up in the slums of Belleville. Each visit requires a phone call to the curator, Bernard Marchois, to book a time for the next afternoon. But this usually means you will have the museum, and M. Marchois, an old friend of Piaf, entirely to yourself.

After a short walk from Père Lachaise or Ménil-montant Métro, you find yourself in the unprepossessing Rue Créspin-du-Gast, down from a Salvation Army refuge. But there is a plaque outside number five for the Musée Les Amis d'Edith Piaf. You dial in the entry codes and ascend four flights of mustard lino in a dark stairwell, fearing increasingly for your life.

Instead, M. Marchois pops out of a door, a man in his

50s with a diamond stud earring, and welcomes you into a sea of memorabilia and kitsch. His hairy peke snuffles at your feet.

The shrine to Piaf consists of two small rooms. The red walls are decorated with original posters from the 1940s and 1950s, tacky oil paintings, and framed letters and cards. There are busts of Piaf, three stage costumes and, splendidly, a life-size cardboard figure of her, less than five feet tall. Her giant teddy bear, of much the same height, sits in a chair by the door. In the background, 'La Vie en Rose' plays on the gramophone.

M. Marchois has every existing Piaf recording – over 300 songs – and will take special requests during the visit. His personal favourite is 'La Foule'. He met Piaf at her apartment in the 16th *arrondissement* in 1958 when he was 16 years old, and continued to be part of her entourage until she died in 1963. 'In real life she was not this sad person of her songs. She was vivacious, fun to be with, always making jokes. We all loved to be around her,' says M. Marchois, who gives his tour in French.

The first time, when a friend took M. Marchois to visit Piaf, he was disappointed. 'He said I would see this great chanteuse, and instead there was this tiny little ordinary woman. But then she sat down at her piano, and I understood.' Thereafter, M. Marchois would visit Piaf almost every night when she was not on tour – 'but she barely spent more than three months of the year in Paris.'

In 1977, all the friends of Edith Piaf gathered souvenirs she had left them and decided to display them to the public. 'There was not much. She was not a great mate-rialist, and only had a few bits of furniture in her big apartment in the 16th.' Now the committee of friends run the Piaf fan club and the museum from the same address in the 11th. Almost 80 per cent of the museum's visitors are young people, all well versed in the Piaf legend. She has also become a major gay icon.

There is something rather Coney Island Sideshow about the atmosphere of the tiny place. Her freaklike size two suede shoes nestle on shelves. The friends also kept obscurities such as a photocopy of Piaf's palm. 'You can see her life line is cut suddenly short here,' says M. Marchois. Piaf died at 48.

Her grave, incidentally, is conveniently near the museum, at the back of Père Lachaise cemetery (plot 97, second row) and is always covered in new flowers. M. Marchois was one of the 400,000 who turned out for the funeral of 'L'Ange Noir' and says 'all Paris mourned'.

1   EDITH PIAF MUSEUM, 5 Rue Créspin-du-Gast, 11th,
      M Ménilmontant, by appointment only, Mon to Thurs afternoon.
      Call Bernard Marchois on 01 43 55 52 72. Free.

❝France's Historic Monument Commission has added the former Aux Belles Poules establishment to the protected list, the first house of ill repute to be so honoured. The brothel is no longer functioning – the shop front at 32 and 34 Rue Blondel has been taken over by Yuwaline Wholesale clothiers, but you can still see the exquisite tiles and murals celebrating turn-of-the-century voluptuousness.

Maurice Rheims, 88-year-old auctioneer, art critic and member of the esteemed Académie Française, warmly remembers similar establishments in the 11th *arrondissement*. 'Leaving adolescence, there was nothing I liked better than to go with friends to one or other of these places. Each had its character – in one there was the literary ambience one finds in Zola, in another, the aesthetic of a Toulouse Lautrec.'

MAILLOL
MUSEUM

What Dina Did

The Musée Maillol's my local, opposite my *boulangerie*, but I would still come across town for its delights. The Maillol[1] is perfectly sized for one thing – a visit is short; it is beautifully sited in the Hôtel Bouchardon, with its dragon waterspouts and pretty courtyard; and its café and changing exhibitions are usually spot on in terms of taste.

The Maillol has a permanent exhibition of the sculptures and paintings of Aristide Maillol, but also of his friends and contemporaries: Bonnard, Gauguin, Matisse, Rousseau and Dufy. Then Maillol's lover and muse, Dina Vierny, championed abstract artists like Poliakoff and Kandinsky, collected Duchamp, and discovered the Russian avant-garde painters, and added them to the mix. The temporary displays in the last few years have included Frieda Kahlo, Diego Rivera, Francis Bacon and Lucian Freud, for which weekend crowds have queued into the street.

Dina Vierny was just 15 when she first met Maillol. For ten years, she remained his model for drawings and sculptures like *La Montagne*, *L'Air* and *La Rivière*, and stayed with him until he was killed in a car accident in 1944. Maillol specialized in unadorned sculptures of large-boned women; the catalogue describes them as having 'a restrained powerfulness, a brimming sensuality beyond any easy effects, a serene and primitive beauty'. They're big girls. His paintings, like the 1941 *Dina Holding a Scarf*, show women full of strength. After the war, Vierny opened a gallery in St Germain, and also began squirrelling works away for the future museum specializing in twentieth-century art.

Her varied tastes and friends made for a fabulous collection: through surrealist André Breton, Vierny met Marcel Duchamp and collected all the editions of his creations. In the museum are Duchamp's bottle rack and bicycle-stool, as well as his *White Box* and snow shovel. She was fond of painters from the naïve school like Douanier Rousseau and de Vivin, and later began making trips to the Soviet Union in the early 1970s. Vierny collected Eric Bulatov's disturbing man-within-man self portrait, and Vladimir Yankilevski's *The Door*, in which a man disappears into a cupboard and then infinity. She also purchased one of the first 'installations' in 1982 (before the concept became so trendy) by Russian Ilya Kabakov. It takes up a whole basement room and is called *The Communal Kitchen*. Battered pots, sieves and spoons sway above your head, lit by bare light bulbs, and the conversation and arguments of the invisible inhabitants play endlessly in the 'domestic gulag'.

Outside, the façade of the museum provides the ultimate bourgeois contrast, with its eighteenth-century fountain of four seasons by Edme Bouchardon. Later, the poet Alfred de Musset lived in the building and, at the end of the war, it passed through a decadent period as La Fontaine des Quatre Saisons jazz cabaret, before returning to more dignified pursuits.

In the vaulted cellar, there is a small café serving
salads and tarts, but I particularly recommended the Fr69
Dina platter: blinis, smoked salmon, crème fraîche and a
shot of Russian vodka.

1 FONDATION DINA VIERNY – MUSÉE MAILLOL, 59 Rue de
   Grenelle, 7th, M Rue du Bac, 01 42 22 59 58, Fr40.

"My son and I went to the Musée Maillol. I prefer
attending museums with a three-year-old because you
only stay an hour and get to go to the café. Children
are discriminating. Matisse's line drawings didn't get a
look-in (dull) whereas his technicolour paintings
generally do. My son favours those close to his own
style: primitivists.

From his point of view, I see things as never before.
He hugs the knees of statues, huge marble thighs and
busts blacking out the light. We study fat, flat toes
instead of facial expressions, because that's what's
available down here.

Duchamp's bicycle wheel on a stool was difficult to
explain – 'not much use', observed my son. I pointed
out Duchamp's urinal and bottle rack; 'Um, it's a loo
and a bottle rack, but because they're behind glass,
they're art.' He gave me a withering stare.

We finished with the Michel Haas temporary exhibition, cave paintings scrapped out of the canvas. 'It
says this guy often paints with his hands,' I told my
son. 'Me too,' he said, pleased.

GUSTAVE
MOREAU
MUSEUM

Symbolism and claustrophobia

The French call them *musées sentimentaux*: collections in the homes of artists and writers which are fascinating as much for the sense of place as the work itself. On page 109, I told you about the Musée Jacquemart-André, which gives the visitor a curious feeling of trespassing on someone else's property.

For visitors coming to Paris for a second or third time, such tasty little obscurities contrast with the large, some-times unpalatable, spread offered by the grand museums. One pleasingly weird discovery is the Musée Gustave Moreau[1], in the symbolist painter's own house in the 9th *arrondissement*, a short walk north of Boulevard Haussmann and a convenient antidote to the department stores.

As Moreau grew old, he dreaded that his works would be dispersed after his death, the whole diluted to insignificance. In the 1890s, he started planning a museum on two floors of his family's home on Rue de la Rochefoucauld. Fortunately, the house was not small, and now displays some 6,000 of his oils, watercolours and drawings.

The best Moreaus are in the symbolist section in the Musée d'Orsay, and *Oedipus and the Sphinx* is in the Metropolitan Museum in New York, but what remains covers every inch of wall space – with grand mythic, Biblical and literary scenes on operatic backgrounds. It is a feast of romantic kitsch, but even those who do not have the highest respect for Moreau's work will still appreciate the World-of-Interiors experience in the private apartments.

The house opened to the public in 1903, although the family apartments were not renovated until 1992. Everything remains intact, however, down to the opposing photographs of Moreau and his mother – of whom he was inordinately fond – and his braided uniform as a member of the Academy of Beaux-Arts. The cramped family apartments on the first floor give some idea of the claustrophobia of the Moreau family – Gustave never married, although he professed his adoration for his friend Alexandrine Dureux. The walls groan with photographs and prints, the light is muted, the china is covered in serpents and stuffed chairs sit in every corner. His deathbed, a grandiose, polished affair, lies in what was the salon.

It is easy to understand how such strange images boiled up in Moreau's imagination and burst out in his painting, given the closeted rooms where he spent his evenings and free time.

Upstairs, two enormous windowed studios display Moreau's works, some paintings 15 feet high, others oddly unfinished. There are stools placed before rotating wooden stands, where literally thousands of framed sketches can be viewed. Moreau wanted to show as much as possible 'so people understand the sum of work and efforts of the artist during his life'. Up a spiral staircase is a second gallery. Guards grudgingly unlock drawers and cupboards filled with small paintings on hinges, layer after layer, and wonderful watercolours which can easily be missed.

There are critics who say Moreau would have made a better writer than a painter, and certainly his literary and artistic styles were both theatrical – in some of the largest oils, the paint is applied with thick, rough brush strokes, or even a spatula, with vague figures scratched into the surface.

His style would not nowadays merit all this space but Moreau's wary eye on posterity has saved this shrine to the bizarre.

1   MUSÉE GUSTAVE MOREAU, 14 Rue de la Rochefoucauld, 9th, M Trinité, 01 48 74 38 50, open Mon, Wed 11am-5pm, other days except Tues 10am-12.45 and 2pm–5pm. Private apartments do not open until noon on Mon and Wed. Fr20.

“Lined up entire family for forced march on the Louvre: it was Sunday, it was going to rain all day, and the apartment seemed increasingly like a padded cell. The inmates' behaviour had left a lot to be desired – the younger prisoner had begun an H-Block protest and was on the (Linus) blanket; the older detainee had objected to the Category-A prisoner plastic cutlery and had gone on hunger strike. A hit of open public space and high-minded culture was required.

We snuck in the Louvre's back entrance underground, laughing at the serpent of tourists waiting 20 damp minutes outside the I.M. Pei Pyramid for security clearance.

Inside, things were worse. The queue for security screening was an hour long, plus a second 15-minute line for tickets.

The *enfants* looked set to stage a riot, until they discovered the Carrousel shopping centre under the Louvre. They abandoned the queue and followed ley lines, instinctive in every child, to the Disney displays in the Virgin Megastore. Then we spent a happy hour there monopolizing the CD-sampling headphones: my one year old headbanged to Megadeth in his pushchair; his brother wouldn't be moved from Enya; and I checked out The Verve (a Wigan band said to be popular with modern youth).

As we headed for the fast-food emporium on the mezzanine, it looked like the Egyptian collection in the new Sackler Wing was slipping from the agenda. My son didn't mind. Turned out he thought he'd been to Egypt anyway although he was suspicious of the Pyramid being glass.

After our Louvre visit descended unexpectedly from high to popular culture, I wondered if other museum goers were forced (intentionally?) into shopping instead. So I called the Louvre press office and told them of the immense tailback. 'Could have been worse,' they said cheerfully. 'On 2 January we had a record-breaking queue of nearly three hours.' They said suffering was shortest on Monday or Wednesday nights, when the museum opens until 10pm.

Of course, some nations fall into line better than others. Recently, an Italian tourist was arrested for assaulting three museum guards who rifled through his

handbag after an excruciatingly long wait. But
Russians, who are flooding into Paris on package
deals, like the gargantuan queues – they bring back
fond memories of the ordered life pre-perestroika.

"When someone half-inched a Corot valued at
£800,000 from the Louvre in broad daylight and with
five guards on duty in that section, I was not at all
surprised. When the Louvre authorities shut all exits
without explanation, and took thousands hostage for
hours, museum regulars shrugged resignedly, while
trapped tourists cried, fainted and had panic attacks.

We regulars know that glasnost and perestroika
have not percolated the Louvre's underground tunnels.
It is still run like GUM, the Soviet department store:
hour-long queues, inexplicable closures, and haughty
officials.

The guards evince a Soviet-style lack of enthusiasm
for the job. I know this because I turned my back in
the Egyptian wing the other day, and a minute later
found my son riding a sphinx.

DELACROIX
MUSEUM

Hidden classical temple in St Germain

The Place de Furstenberg, off Boulevard St Germain, is beautiful, with cobbles and broadleafed trees, and just off the square is Eugène Delacroix's old workshop and apartment, one of the most charming small museums in Paris.

Delacroix is immediately recognizable as the man on the back of the Fr100 note, and as one of France's finest nineteenth-century painters. His major works, including *The 28th of July*, *Algerian Women*, *The Prisoner of Chillon*, *Don Juan*, *Jewish Musicians* and *The Death of Sardanapale* are in the Louvre. The little Musée Delacroix[1] is more about the atmosphere of a Left Bank studio than about his grandest works – there are a few oil portraits, but mostly sketches and studies are on show. The artist moved to Rue Furstenberg in 1857 towards the end of his life, when he found himself exhausted by the walk from his old apartment to the church of St Sulpice, where he was painting one of the chapels. His rooms were not large but there was a walled garden where he decided to build a studio. By this time he was well established and not short of cash, so the result is more a classical temple than a garden shed.

Like many people, Delacroix had trouble with his

builders, and waited eight months before his studio was ready. 'Half the workmen aren't reliable,' he moaned, 'and the other half are lazy or too expensive .. . . this has caused great annoyance.' The eventual result was a cream, stone building with a frieze over the front door and enormous windows and skylights.

Delacroix came to find his apartment delightful, with its view at the front over a cobbled courtyard and the flowerboxes of his neighbours and behind over his garden, which is still a place where visitors can sit and escape the bustle of the boulevards.

He lived with his longtime housekeeper, Jenny Le Guillou, and there are two portraits of her – one as a young girl with an unfortunate snub nose, and later as a mature woman, grave in a bonnet.

In the hall, there is an enormous bust of Delacroix with pointy moustache and demi-beard. A foppish scarf falls from his neck. His paintings and sketches are displayed in what was once his bedroom, library and salon. A few pieces of his furniture are dotted about, but the most interesting is his metal-lined mahogany painting table in the studio. In glass cases there are his original palettes, still thick with carefully ranged paint.

There are also letters to friends, such as the writer George Sand and Baudelaire, who wrote a poem in honour of the painter, perhaps referring to his gloomy backgrounds: 'Delacroix, lake of blood/Haunted by wicked angels/Shaded by a wood of evergreen pines'.

The Delacroix museum is a pleasant stop on a wander around St Germain, where he lived until his death at home in 1863. From here it is a five-minute walk to St Sulpice past the Marché St Germain. In the church, he worked on the Saints-Anges chapel for more than a decade, and there are two more paintings.

The Delacroix Left Bank tour can be completed with a coffee in the Café de la Mairie, opposite St Sulpice, where, no doubt, Delacroix occasionally took lunch.

1   MUSÉE DELACROIX, 6 Rue Furstenberg, 6th, M St Germain, 01 44 41 86 50. Open daily 10am-5pm, except Tues, Fr15.

ZADKINE
MUSEUM
Secret garden

Out of the back gate of the Luxembourg Gardens, down a little alley, lies the secret garden of Ossip Zadkine.¹ You hear cooing doves before you enter the gates, and inside there's something closer to a cottage than an urban museum, with an ivy-walled garden, a fig tree and a riot of flowers in summer. Statues hang out on the little lawn and behind bushes; you surprise them as you wander in.

Whether Zadkine was the greatest of sculptors is another question, but this should not detract from your pleasure in his garden, house and airy studio off the Rue d'Assas. He arrived in Paris as a 19-year-old from Russia, stayed at the nearby Rue Vaugirard, had some works included in the Salon des Independents, and then enlisted as a stretcher bearer for the First World War. It was not until the 1920s and 1930s that his works began to gain recognition; in 1932 he made the Venice Biennial.

His early sculptures were primitivist – he admired Gauguin – in rough wood and stone reminiscent of African carvings. Then his lines smoothed, the faces and arms elongated, paralleling his friendship with Modigliani. In 1920, he married Valentine Prax, a painter, and formed a late attachment to cubism. His sculptures followed suit, becoming increasingly geometric. But you can see, even from his surroundings, that he was more lyrical and naturalist at heart, and strict form fell by the wayside by the time he found this space in the Rue d'Assas in 1928. He never left, except to escape Nazi persecution of Jews during the war, when he travelled to America. Prax was left to shut up the studio. 'With the help of the maid's husband, I moved the bronzes into various people's cellars in the Rue d'Assas, and I disguised the worth of ten of them by covering them in coal dust.' Zadkine returned to find the place virtually unchanged, retrieved the sculptures, and worked on until he died in 1967. He is buried in Montparnasse cemetery nearby.

He had a sizeable studio, but he often tackled larger sculptures in his garden. After his death, Prax wrote: 'There, in the open air, Zadkine worked with granite and Pollinay stone as well as hardwoods. He gave the impression of being a workman in his grey corduroy suit and his brown leather cap. He also wore huge goggles to protect his eyes from chips of wood or granite.'

Inside, the house which was filled with clutter by Prax, has been gutted to leave white walls and plain windows which display the statues at their best. His thunder-thighed *Venus Caryatid* stands in the alcove of the garden door. There are temporary exhibitions too; one recently dealt with the centrality of trees and wood in modern art and sculpture, perfect for the setting. A five-foot ball of sequoia wood rolled on the lawn, there were photographs of trees pierced with giant hoop earrings, plus forested Klees and Giacomettis.

1   MUSÉE ZADKINE, 100 bis Rue d'Assas, 6th, M Vavin,
     01 43 26 91 90. Closed Mon. Fr17.50.

LOVERS' PARIS

THE FRENCH KISS

Traditional Sites

We all come here with Robert Doisneau's black and white photograph *The Kiss at l'Hôtel de Ville* trapped in our heads. You know it from poster shops everywhere: the young man has rumpled James-Deanish hair, and he's still holding the remains of his cigarette between finger and thumb. It's the 1950s, so she's more refined and twinsetted, but her head is thrown back with the passion of the moment. Cars and people pass in blurs, but the couple are frozen together.

The city does, somehow, encourage public kissing like none other. Young couples can take a good three minutes, briefcases and tongues entangled, to take leave of one another as they go to work in the Métro in the morning. Bridges over the Seine, particularly in warm weather, cause kissers to multiply like bacteria, and high points – the Eiffel Tower, Notre Dame, the roof of the Samaritaine department store – bring on high fever. Best of all, no one minds. Parisians smile just a little, and pass by.

Kissing has been elevated from a merely physical activity to an art, in terms of siting and atmosphere. No ordinary street corner will do when you can enlist as background the steps of the Opéra, the private (two-seater) dining-rooms at Laperouse, or a Rodin sculpture – *The Kiss*, of course.

Most usefully, a book has now been published on the subject: *Où s'embrasser à Paris*[1]. Even for non-French speakers, it provides a host of addresses for the act, and a series of symbols for each site: the most romantic time of the day; the best time of the year; and whether kisses should be long or discreet. Chapter 1, 'Les Grands Classiques' includes Doisneau's famous site, but explains that to precisely reproduce the picture, your lips should meet over at the Café de l'Hôtel de Ville at the table just under the 'C' of Café.

Another classic is on the Pont Neuf straddling the Ile de la Cité, and for increased privacy you can take the steps down to the Square de Vert-Galant. The Pont Neuf is also the city's most popular suicide point, perhaps because of those romantic memories. There's a tradition that you can make a wish while going under the Pont Marie, but you should not reveal it to the person with you in the *bâteau mouche*, or batobus. The tree-shaded Place de Furstenburg on the Left Bank, after a public odyssey at the cafés de Flore and Deux Magots, is a quiet, beautiful spot for a long snog. The book recommends that you remain standing.

For those mad with love, tumultuous passions can be cooled in summer in the lion fountain at St Sulpice or the Fontaine St Michel. Fantasists can kiss before the altar of a church; St Julien le Pauvre is said to be particularly romantic, or there is the clinch in the changing room of a wedding dress shop (preferably the Fr400 satin creations at the tacky Tati).

Any serious couple will have their favourite film in mind, be it Beneix's *Diva* (take the stage at the Théâtre du

Châtelet once the audience has left), Isabelle Adjani in *Subway* (RER station Auber) or *Last Tango in Paris*, where a punch-up ends in passion on the platform of Bir-Hakeim Métro.

A mere guidebook can go no further, but it is worth remembering Guy de Maupassant's words in *Le Baiser*: 'The kiss is only a preface, however. But it is a charming preface, more delicious than the work of art itself.'

1   *Où s'embrasser à Paris*, Parigramme, Fr35.

"On fine afternoons I practise my French comprehension in the Jardin du Luxembourg: I lurk on benches and eavesdrop. My best snoop so far was when I came upon a man and a woman – she in fur, he in cashmere – of an indeterminate age. They were holding hands, so they were obviously not married, but both wore wedding rings. Her voice rose a little, as did my radar from behind an English magazine: 'He read the bill from France Telecom, showing the first four numbers of every single call. Yours was there – every day. Do you think he noticed?' The man made reassuring noises and anxiously lit a cigarette. 'What about the credit-card print-out? And the hire car?' More reassurance. 'And I heard a terrible thing . . .' Other bench-occupants began to listen in, too. 'That hotels automatically send out Christmas cards to their guests from that year. What if one arrives?'

Thereafter, she began to mumble darkly, but the problem was clear: a French man or woman's inalienable right to take a lover was under a threat –

from new technology. The traditional *cinq à sept*, the two-hour tryst after work, the secret weekends away, might be no more. As computers print out every purchase, every detail of private life, with a time and a date, and plastic cards replace the discretion of cash, a grand French tradition is being menaced – by electronic lipstick on the collar.

COCKTAILS

Le long drink in town

After a long and dusty day marching the streets of Paris in pursuit of culture, it is essential to take the cocktail hour seriously. The break between sightseeing and dinner is important for whetting the appetite and calming the nerves. Le long drink, as they say here, should take place in the city, but as far from the bustle and traffic as possible.

The cafés along the great boulevards are pleasant enough, but do not soothe the wearied traveller. Instead, head for some of the newer hotels and cafés with outdoor terraces in the city centre which provide people-watching without the discomfort of street life.

The most splendid of these is the Hôtel Costes[1] on Rue St Honoré. Two discreet banners mark the entrance between expensive shops, and you walk into a dimly lit orange corridor with an oriental carpet. This leads into sumptuous little lounges and lobbies filled with a mixture of curious Victoriana, Napoleon III sofas, befringed silk chairs and parlour palms.

Beyond, in sudden daylight is the courtyard, reminiscent of an Italian villa, the walls painted terracotta with pale green windows and balustrades featuring Romanesque statues. Among the potted orange trees, under cream umbrellas lined with red there are tables where one can order an expensive glass of champagne or a Kir.

It is worth nursing this drink for some time in order to observe the comings and goings of grand Americans and rich Eurotrash. Last time I wandered in, there were Italians in sharkskin suits with extensive lapels, dealing and back slapping. At another table, a French girl with exquisite cheekbones filed her nails, awaiting what turned out to be a much older and smaller man. Even the waitresses themselves, columns of femininity draped in the latest Gucci dresses, were worth watching. When a mobile phone went off, five different people searched their bags and pockets.

The Costes is the only hotel in Paris at the moment for the fashion set, and during the shows, people-watching reaches its peak. The hotel was decorated by Jacques Garcia. Previously the Costes brothers used designer Philippe Starck to create their famous Café Costes in Les Halles.

Starck addicts can take themselves over to Café Marly[2] for the cocktail hour, set in the colonnades of the Louvre overlooking the Pyramid. Again, there is the outdoor setting without traffic. During the day, Café Marly is so-so, packed with international museum-goers, but in the evening, the French and the chic arrive and the place is transformed. There are Starck chairs and long banquettes covered in red with white piping behind the stone balustrades where kings once paced. Cocktails are F65, but sharing a bottle of wine for F100 is a better, longer-lasting option.

On Monday and Wednesday nights, the Louvre opens part of its permanent collection until 9.45pm, and temporary exhibitions open until 10pm, except Tuesday (check as times can vary), so it is possible to spend a civilized, uncrowded hour among the paintings, before repairing to the café. Inside, the decor is also extraordinary, with red and black laquered walls featuring gold symbols, a ridiculous chandelier and comfortable velvet-covered chairs and sofas. The food at Café Marly is better for a snack than dinner.

Creeping further outdoors, without leaving central Paris, is the Café Véry[3] in the Jardin des Tuileries near the Jeu de Pomme. There are four other cafés in the Tuileries, which are little more than ice-cream and soda stalls. Café Véry can be differentiated by its posher chairs and its strange wooden-shuttered pagoda building. The Tuileries has this quantity of cafés because those who walk its white dust paths on a summer day or the frozen wind-blown wastes in winter find themselves instantly parched, feeling in the blinding light that they have traversed a tract of desert, not formal park. The best succour is to be had under the shade of the chestnut trees at Café Véry, which does a Kir with muscadet for F16, and chilled Normandy cider for F13.

You still can't fault the cocktails or the service at the Hemingway Bar[4] in the Ritz, although the prices are less relaxing. The ancient standby, where the Bloody Mary was invented in 1921, remains Harry's Bar[5], near the Opéra. It's all wood panelling, university pennants and shields, beer-soaked air, and perfectly executed Martinis.

The modern version of all this is the water bar in Colette[6], the designer store on Rue St Honoré. They serve alcohol too until 7pm, but anyone seriously hip drinks mineral water, including St Georges, a Corsican blend in a bottle designed by the ubiquitous Philippe Starck. Colette

styledesignartfood, to give it the full title, offers 50 different mineral waters, from Lynx Elite, 'which stimulates the
digestion', to Rosé de la Reine, which is 'bio-electric,' and
the ominous-sounding Montez Gaz from Austria.

Colette is said to be *très tendance*, but which Parisian
buys the Space Food ice-cream in silver packets (sell by
2002), the trendoid English magazines such as *Wallpaper*, or
the clothes from Alexander McQueen? There is only one
video on sale: *Trainspotting*, of course. The best items – you
might call them jewellery – are rubber bands. Normally
available from stationers, these are now bracelets printed
with the words TREASON, FEAR, DESPAIR or PLAGIARISM –
the last one a fun anonymous gift for one's colleagues.

1   HOTEL COSTES, 239 Rue St Honoré, 1st, M Concorde,
    01 42 44 50 00.
2   CAFÉ MARLY, 93 Rue de Rivoli, Louvre, 1st, M Louvre-Rivoli,
    01 49 26 06 60.
3   CAFÉ VÉRY, Jardin des Tuileries, 1st, M Tuileries, 01 47 03 94 84.
4   HEMINGWAY BAR, Ritz Hotel, Place Vendôme, 1st, M Concorde,
    01 43 16 30 30.
5   HARRY'S BAR, 5 Rue Danou, 2nd, M Opéra, 01 42 61 71 14.
6   COLETTE, 213 Rue St Honoré, 1st, M Tuileries, 01 42 86 91 03.

❝Not easy living on a thin street in a thin
arrondissement of a thin town, where even Brooke
Shields is criticized for having the arms of a *déménageur*
– a furniture mover. Thus the pressure to follow the
latest *Elle* magazine fruit-and-veg diet is great, but can
only be borne if one interprets wine as a form of fruit.
Better still is the diet booklet free with *Biba*
magazine, which gives seriously Epicurean advice.
'Choose a slice of *foie gras* at 180 calories, rather than

50g of *rillettes* [fatty pâté] at 240 cal' it begins, not even considering readers who prefer to toy with the latest lettuce. Gastronomes will be glad to know that fresh goats' cheese has half the calories of packaged stuff, and that the slimmer should favour duck breast over *confit de canard*, onion tart over quiche Lorraine.

Only in France would dieters be given useful counsel for *l'heure de l'apéro* – cocktail hour. One should avoid the peanuts and favour green olives, at six calories, over black at 15. Better still, red wine is an encouraging 62 calories, compared with Pernod at 265.

SINGLE IN THE CITY

La chasse

A British student who helped with the research on this book was 20, lived in the Bastille, and had no need to look for Frenchmen, for they dogged her every step, whistled, and accosted her in the street, cafés and bookshops, until she was forced to flee forever on the Eurostar. Some of us are not so fortunate, however, and must place ourselves in the way of such harassment.

One cliché – which is generally true – is that Frenchmen are not backward in coming forward; give them a centimetre and they'll take a kilometre. Thus to aid *la chasse* you need only appear – preferably with a friend, for they hunt in numbers – in the correct hot spots. French women are harder quarry, spoiled by the quality of service and seduction by their compatriots, although they may still be charmed by a foreigner over coffee up at the safety of the zinc.

Men throughout the world favour the same natural habitats. In Paris, the basement of the BHV department store[1] in the Marais, filled with drill-bits, saws, widgits and muscly (though perhaps dull) men is good hunting territory. You need only ask questions about superior shelving, before the *bricoleur*, or DIY enthusiast, will be offering to put it up *chez toi*. It is said the bed department of Ikea is worth prowling too on Saturdays or Sundays.

Another sure-fire hit is Décathlon[2], the mega sports shop at the Madeleine, where you can select a jogger or tennis player along with some new training shoes. Wine merchants, and the large *foires du vin* that come every year to the city, have richer pickings, in terms of the per capita income of your quarry. Displaying ignorance or knowledge of the vintages is equally efficacious.

Obviously it's hard to carry off the *bricoleur* or wine-buying deception if you're merely in Paris for the week. Instead, the traditional bookshops, record shops like the Virgin Megastore[3] and exhibitions should be considered for meetings with either sex. For British or bilingual types, Brentanos[4] or W.H. Smith[5] (particularly on Sunday afternoons) have proved friendly zones. Any shop in the giant Fnac[6] book and record chain should also be recommended, for management policy encourages people to hang around without buying. If your tastes run to something more intellectual and Left Banky, there is late-night La Hune[7] which arranges its philosophy and psychiatry books by letter, so you can cruise the K shelves if you desire a Kantian, F for a Freudian. In the Marais, Les Mots à la Bouche[8] has a gay and lesbian clientele.

For exhibitions, a little knowledge goes a long way, for you should be able to say something appropriate about the installation or sculpture when you start the conversation. Sunday mornings are said to be best for this, when couples are still in bed. Carry a paper napkin in your pocket and eyeliner pencil, so you can casually scribble down your phone number for the innocent victim.

1   BHV, 52 Rue de Rivoli, 4th, M Hôtel-de-Ville, 01 42 74 90 00.
2   DECATHLON, 17 Boulevard de la Madeleine, 1st, M Madeleine,
       01 55 35 97 55.
3   VIRGIN MEGASTORE, 52 Avenue des Champs-Elysées, 8th,
       M Franklin D. Roosevelt, 01 49 53 50 00.
4   BRENTANOS, 37 Avenue de l'Opéra, 2nd, M Opéra, 01 42 61 52 50.
5   W.H. SMITH, 248 Rue de Rivoli, 1st, M Concorde, 01 44 77 88 99.
6   FNAC, 74 Avenue des Champs-Elysées, 8th, M Franklin D. Roosevelt,
       01 53 53 64 64.
7   LA HUNE, 170 Boulevard St Germain, 6th, M St Germain,
       01 45 48 35 85.
8   LES MOTS À LA BOUCHE, 6 Rue St Croix de la Brétonnerie,
       4th, M Hôtel-de-Ville, 01 42 78 88 30.

"Seems that the lesson of Dumas's beautiful courtesan in *La Dame aux Camélias* holds – it's still attractive to be ill. I was walking to the office in mid-winter, nursing a cold and performing my hacking tubercular cough every two minutes, when an elegant man in a leather jacket stopped me. 'That doesn't sound good,' he said, smiling sympathetically. 'You should stop smoking, you know.' I stormed past. I haven't smoked since I was 18. Worse still, a complete stranger used the intimate *tu* to me. I moaned about the insult to a native: 'Silly,' she said. 'Didn't you realize that's a pick-up line?'

CULTURAL PARIS

CHURCH CONCERTS

Trumpets at Sainte-Chapelle

When King Louis IX built Sainte-Chapelle in 1248 he did not have its use as a public concert hall in mind. Indeed, he found the lower orders so repulsive that he created a church in the basement of Sainte Chapelle so that the servants would not worship alongside royalty.

Now, however humble your origins, you can spend the evening in the grandest possible manner in this church on the Ile de la Cité being serenaded by some of France's best classical musicians. An increasing number of churches in Paris are opening their doors in the evening to classical music, and the experience is certainly superior to that of a dull municipal concert hall.

On a Sunday night we went to hear *The Trumpets of Versailles* at Sainte-Chapelle, in the same building as the Palais de Justice and the Conciergerie. Instead of queueing for entry during the day with Euro-coach parties desperate to gawp at Marie Antoinette's cell, evening visitors can wander through the marbled corridors of the palace. At night the church was free from dictatorial tourist guides – instead, there was a well-mannered rustle of anticipation and only French voices to be heard.

When the lights were lowered, with just a spotlight over the trumpeters and the organist before the altar, the church became as it was meant to be seen, not in electric glare but in half-darkness.

Although the magnificent stained glass disappeared, the pillars painted red and gold, or blue with fleur-de-lys, suddenly glowed. The gold stars glinted on the blue arched ceiling – 50 feet high and an architectural marvel in itself – and carved wooden apostles seemed to move on their pedestals.

The trumpeters played Handel, Telemann and Vivaldi, the organist a Bach prelude and fugue, while the audience was lulled into a swoon by the atmosphere and the music.

Louis IX was extremely religious and created Saint-Chapelle to house the Crown of Thorns and the other relics that he acquired from the Emperor of Constantinople, at a price said to be three times the cost of the actual building work. In medieval times the church was known as 'a gateway to heaven'. It is also a gateway to some of the city's best classical concerts several times a week.

The economics make sense, too – why pay Fr40 to be pushed through Sainte-Chapelle with a bunch of tourists when, for Fr90 or Fr150, you can luxuriate in the same surroundings for a two-hour concert?

The church concerts are advertised in the *Pariscope* listings magazine, published every Wednesday. So long as you turn up half an hour beforehand, most tickets can be bought at the door.

In an average week there might be Russian Orthodox songs from a St Petersburg ensemble at Sainte-Chapelle; Bach, Corette and Handel played on flute and organ at the Eglise des Bilettes; a cello soloist at Eglise St Julien le

Pauvre; the Lyons choir at St Louis en Ile, plus Purcell and Scarlatti played at the American church.

The decision as to which concert to attend depends on both the architectural and the musical desires of the party. Concerts at the Madeleine may lack the intimacy of, say, Sainte-Chapelle, but they certainly make up for it in grandeur tending more to orchestral than chamber music.

The cavernous inside of the Madeleine is particularly lavish with marble and gilt, and the musicians play before Charles Marochetti's *Mary Magdalene Ascending to Heaven* behind the high altar and candlesticks.

St Germain des Prés, the city's oldest church, also has regular concerts and some free organ recitals. The church is an extraordinary mish-mash of sixth-century Gothic and Romanesque architecture, and there are those who swear that the low lighting and soft music do much to improve it.

The bookshop chain FNAC and the Virgin Megastore under the Louvre sell tickets for church concerts, otherwise call the *Pariscope* listing.

PERE
LACHAISE

A place to be seen dead in

Père Lachaise[1], now Paris's most prestigious cemetery, had a rather unpromising start. When it opened in 1804 on a hill inconveniently far from town, it was treated with disdain by Parisians, and no one who was anyone would be seen dead there.

By 1815, a mere 2,000 citizens were six feet under in Père Lachaise, and the lack of cortèges traipsing up the hill was most worrying for the administrators. Something had to be done, and it was thus that the first public relations campaign started to attract the dead. The cemetery got hold of the bodies of La Fontaine and Molière and placed them in the same enclosure in stone sarcophagi. That covered potential clients with a literary bent. Then the Gothic tomb where Abélard and Heloïse were reunited in 1701 was procured, bringing in young lovers by the dozen on pilgrimages.

By the 1830s, there were over 30,000 tombs, and the craze for Père Lachaise was sealed when Honoré de Balzac had all of the characters in his novels buried there. In 1850, Balzac joined his fictional characters in person, his tomb topped by a gigantic bust showing his trendily bobbed haircut.

Today, Père Lachaise boasts the best collection of

notables in town, including Frédéric Chopin, Sarah Bernhardt, Jim Morrison, Edith Piaf, Guillaume Apollinaire, Eugène Delacroix, Oscar Wilde, Dominique Ingrès, Anthelme Brillat-Savarin, Yves Montand, the early photographer Nadar, and Gertrude Stein (with Alice B. Toklas modestly added on the back of the tombstone).

Cemetery-goers need to be well equipped for the pilgrimage. The maps in most guidebooks are too small, so it is worth buying a full map, F10 from any of the flower shops near the cemetery gates or by Père Lachaise Métro. One of the worst guidebooks is *Une heure au Père Lachaise*, which provides little information beyond the map and, as anyone will discover, it takes two hours for even a minimal tour of the century. Better to rely on the map and your own choice of the famous.

The shady Père Lachaise is a wonderful place to sit, and was designed by the architect of the Bourse, Alexandre Brongniart. It has over 5,000 trees, winding paths, little staircases and grand squares – none of that dull mathematical look of modern cemeteries. The furthest graves are a 20-minute walk to the top of the hill, so it is worth bringing water or drinks for a much-needed rest stop. Finding graves is by no means as simple as it looks on the map. You will often have to search through a couple of rows back from the paths, and the staff are somewhat unhelpful.

The best is often to be found just mooching around, sneaking into tombs with stained glass windows and mysterious sculpture. Best graves, however, include the Pharonic version of Oscar Wilde sculpted by Jacob Epstein, inscrutable and grumpy, as well you might look if you had been shunned by England, and not made particularly welcome in France after imprisonment.

The grave of Victor Noir features a life-size, realistic sculpture of the journalist sleeping flat on top of the grave with his top hat thrown off casually beside him, his high-heeled boots protruding over the edge of the stone. In the same section as Edith Piaf, buried as Madame Lamboukas with her young Greek lover, are extraordinary sculptures commemorating the victims of Nazi concentration camps, modern and chilling against comforting Gothic-revival and Victoriana.

The grave titled intimately 'Fred Chopin' receives 800 visitors a day, and has not only the female muse of music sitting on a pedestal by Clesinger, but also a creepy bas-relief of Chopin's profile which was taken from a cast a few minutes after his death.

Up at the back near the chimneys of the crematorium is the tomb of singer and actor Yves Montand, scene of a ghoulish investigation in 1998, when his supposed daughter insisted his body was exhumed to test for DNA. The tests proved negative, but exhumations are on the increase.

The busiest grave is that of The Doors' singer Jim Morrison. At the moment, you can barely see the inscription at all, because the area round the tomb has been roped off. The anonymous marble bust of Morrison, with the open mouth that visitors would tuck a cigarette in, has been removed.

Two guards stand by with walkie-talkies on anti-hippy patrol, ending the tradition of having a joint and a bottle of cheap wine at the graveside.

After visiting Père Lachaise, it seems unfair to ignore Mère Lachaise, a pleasant, funky, plant-filled café for the living just down the road on Boulevard de Menilmontant.

1 PERE LACHAISE, Boulevard de Menilmontant, 20th, M Père
   Lachaise or Philippe Auguste, open daily 8am-5.30pm, longer in
   summer.
2 MERE LACHAISE, 78, Boulevard de Menilmontant, 20th,
   01 47 97 61 60.

"The French way of death is becoming somewhat lively.
As Molière pointed out, 'One only dies once, and it's
for such a long time', so why should one rest in peace
under an uninspiring slab of granite? Before going to
meet their Maker, chic Parisians are meeting art
undertakers to decide on an appropriate monument to
their lives. Under an old viaduct in the 12th *arrondissement*, the Gallery of Funeral Art has just opened. In the
window are wrought-iron sculptures of the silhouettes
of lovers, urns shaped like pagodas, teapots in multi-
coloured ceramics and even grave mobiles, perhaps to
ease the boredom.

Forty artists have provided 'revolutionary
interpretations' of death, which start at Fr2,500 – a
better long-term investment that a top-of-the-line teak
coffin lined with purple silk and a frilly pillow, which,
like a wedding dress, is only seen once.

Pierre Aubert, the owner, talks of the 'reintegration
of death into the collective conscience' and says his
objective is to diminish grief: 'We are there to break
the monotony and explain to families that they have
the right to construct their own monuments.' But
some families may find his latest suggestion a little too
macabre: a desktop hourglass filled with the Loved
One's ashes, instead of sand, to mark time.

"During Toussaint, the All Saints' Day holiday – now sponsored by chrysanthemum growers – your average French family runs up a big florist's bill and picnics with a bottle of wine at the graves of Loved Ones. Observing this, it struck me how pleasant it would be to be buried in Paris. One's mates would have an annual excuse to get on the Eurostar to pay their respects and eat in particularly good brasseries, and one could waste away in the company of Sartre and de Beauvoir at Montparnasse.

I began investigations on behalf of myself and those readers who would prefer to avoid burial in Penge or East Grinstead. Turns out there are no residence requirements – you only have to breathe your last in Paris to get long-term residency. If you book early, all the really baroque and weird Paris cemeteries still have space – apart from Calvaire on the hill of Montmartre. 'Eternity' is variously defined in France, depending on price. A 'perpetual' grave site in Père Lachaise will cost from £1,200 to £7,000 depending upon architecture and location. A 50-year rental costs a minimum of £600, and ten years is a snip at £110. But what happens when the right to afterlife storage runs out? At Père Lachaise, they pop you in their ossuary for time immemorial, and after a polite four-year interval, they rent out your ancient mausoleum or gravestone to some other stiff. Best to go for the 'perpetual' option then: although £7,000 may seem a lot, when you consider what you pay per square metre for apartments here, it's a bargain.

PHILOSOPHERS' CAFES

Socrates and a double espresso

Sunday morning at the voguish Café des Phares[1] in the Bastille. By 11 o'clock no one can get through the doors, so thick is the crowd. Customers, smoking ferociously, pass notes above people's heads to order double espressos. The chatter rises with anticipation. Then the messiah appears, walking through the crowd parted by a waiter wearing a shirt logoed: 'A Café for Socrates'.

One of Paris's many hip philosopher professors is here to lead a Sunday brunch for the mind. He perches on a high stool; combining the skills of game-show host and intellectual, he rounds up subjects for this morning's great philosophical debate over the croissants. 'Utopia what's the point?' suggests one woman. 'The morality of the nuclear tests,' says a man grabbing the microphone. 'Only the unique is Other,' proffers another. This is philosophy for the punters, by the punters.

Café philosophy is the rage. This week, amateur existentialists and determinists can attend 13 debates in *les bistros philos* across Paris.

Hélène d'Alançon has been coming to the debates for four months. 'I began to feel a need to reflect, to think about something profound.' A 38-year-old librarian, she has started reading 'books I would never dare touch before'. 'And', she grins, 'you meet people here.'

Further along is a splendid leather jacket containing Micham Charif, a 35-year-old documentary-maker. 'This is the way cafés used to be. You could walk in the door and talk politics with someone, anyone. It was a great French tradition,' he says.

The prof brings everyone to order: 'We will discuss "Only the unique is Other".' Several people order Camparis and beer, suspecting only an unconstrained mind will cope with this concept.

At the front, spotty students jockey for the microphone, while further away, the middle aged take careful notes of the prof's great words and plot clever one-liners. The crowd picks at the meanings of 'unique' and 'Other' as though they were scabs. Kind people explain chunks of the argument for me, until I realize that it often makes no sense in French or English.

'That's the whole point,' the prof suggests later. 'It's a phrase from the Jewish philosopher Levinas, and if a great philosopher can produce something so unclear, then that should make us think about all glib statements.'

There is no great obstacle, other than the lack of cafés, to prevent philosophy spreading to Britain. 'The Eurostar will permit us to make some raids on London and perhaps we can speed things up a bit.' The prof says Britain has a reputation more for analytical than moral philosophy, and it is moral questions that really interest people.

The subjects for debate are often far from lofty. They have included: 'Should one spit in the soup?' (during strikes), Joslein Gaarder's bestseller *Sophie's World*, and 'Is defenestration a philosophical act?' (after the suicide of a French philosopher). The debates at the Café des Phares began casually in 1992. Philosophy, say the café-thinkers, has a role to play in the divides between rich and poor, the growth of technology and the threatening of democracy. 'Philosophy gives reason a chance. It is a chance to stay on the riverbank and not be swept away on the river of super-stition which will lead to hate, passion and passivity,' goes the creed at Les Phares.

There are simpler explanations. In an article in the *Magazine Litteraire*, Dominique Folschied, professor of Philosophy at the University of Marne-la-Vallée, puts it more succinctly: '*La philosophie est à la mode.*'

1   CAFÉ DES PHARES, 7 Place de la Bastille, 4th, M Bastille,
     01 42 72 04 70, debates 11am Sunday.
    Also at CAFÉ DE FLORE, 188 Boulevard St Germain, 6th,
     M St Germain, 01 45 48 06 93, debates first Wed of each month in
     English.

«What could be more quintessentially Eurotrash than a philosophical debate, in English, in a French café? Especially when it's the Café de Flore, home to existential tourism and the most expensive hot chocolate on the Left Bank. Here, in this cradle of pretentious gittery, Paris's finest expat thinkers meet once a month to dissect topics such as: 'Does fate exist?'; 'Is maturity necessary?'; and this evening's 'Are beliefs borne out of the limitations of our intelligence?'

Upstairs in the Flore, etiolated students in military jackets, ladies of a certain age in crisp linen, and

bohemians with beards compete for intellectual space.
Holding the floor is Gale Prawda, an American doctor
of philosophy who came to Paris in 1968 and never
left. She's also an Anglo-French 'philosophy
entrepreneur' who has brought the system to cafés in
London, and is unembarrassed by the idea of T-shirts
saying: 'Café Philo at the Café de Flore'.

After I order a Kir to see me through the
post-Kierkegaardian worst, I realize I'm the only
person in the room drinking. Everyone else is on
coffee or Perrier. I bail out. Downstairs, drunks are
philosophizing: upstairs, the would-be philosophers
seem perilously close to 12-step recovery.

Back in the dipsomaniac days of Jean-Paul, Simone,
Arthur and Albert, philosophy at the Flore was never
this dry. As one biog notes: 'After too much liquor,
Sartre became bellicose and refused to let himself be
put into a car to go home. One night Koestler
slammed a taxi door in Camus's face, leaving him with
a black eye. Camus became irritable when drinking,
and Koestler undertook to seduce de Beauvoir.'

❝Just been reading the philosophy paper for the
Baccalauréat exams. Scary. 'Is the value of a theory
dependent on its practical efficacy? Is man by nature
neither morally good or bad? Can you describe an act
as inhuman?' Apparently the average 17-year-old can
answer these 'with reference to Comte, Hegal, Kant
or Aristotle' rather than Natalie Imbruglia.

So where does the French adolescent get to grips
with great minds? At the café, at the gym and in *Vogue*
magazine, of course. We've just discussed philosophy

cafés. 'Philo' gym, however, is new. The existential
exercises conducted by Davina at the Compagnie
Bleue sports clubs are described as 'a collective
experience which allows you to acquire greater self-
knowledge in a friendly and sharing atmosphere'. For
the lazy, *Vogue* has a monthly 'Philo' page, proving high
heels don't mean low intelligence. She may look like a
fashion victim, but inside the *Vogue* reader is wondering: 'What gender is *la philo*? Male or female'? It
seems the question remains as difficult as defining the
sex of angels.

OPERA UNVEILED

Garnier's folly

The Opéra[1] is perhaps the most fabulously camp and over-the-top building in Paris. The ego of Charles Garnier, its architect, was unbounded, to the extent he placed busts of himself and his wife in the grand halls, and fixed his initials everywhere, like a vulgar spray painter. Garnier's philosophy was more – is more – with knobs on. Statues of Pegasus prance across the roof, too high for anyone to really see, stone lions and eagles festoon the windows and every crenellation has a curlicue. This was a guy, you feel, who thought it was Christmas every day, and not always in the best of taste.

Inside, the excess is equal. Most days at 1pm there is an Opéra tour in French[2]. Even if you don't understand everything, it does gain you access to boxes and back doors that are denied to the public. First, you are confronted by the grand staircase, in multiple marbles, with steps 32 feet wide. It is still haunted by the swishing silks of the *haute bourgeoisie*, for the point of the Opéra then was more social than musical. The Opéra was a pinnacle of the Second Empire, designed in 1858 for Napoleon III. Unfortunately, the Commune and Siege intervened, and Napoleon died before the 14 years of work was completed. He was never able to drive his horses and carriage up the ornate ramp into his personal indoor stable on the first-floor Rue Scribe entrance which led directly to the royal box, avoiding potential assassins and riff-raff.

The guide takes you up and up into the gods and sneaks you into the back row, where the ballet is rehearsing in grubby sweats, and you watch the leaps and hear the thuds, undrowned by a tinny piano. It's very atmospheric. Most of the opera is now performed at the new building in the Bastille, but the ballet, perversely, has remained at the Opéra. The fantastic auditorium has been refurbished in a riot of gilt and red, restoring the original (rewoven) 'Trianon' velvet upholstery, and the gondola seats in the boxes, with a choice of one arm or two. With the heavy gold pillars towering and decorative icing dripping from the boxes, you feel as if you're trapped inside a giant wedding cake. The style can best be described as Roman, Rococo and Hodge Podge.

Then you look up, and there's the round ceiling painted by Marc Chagall in 1964 as a gift to the city, with 12 crazy scenes, some inspired by ballets like *The Firebird* and *Swan Lake*. The guide explains that Chagall did not hang on a trapeze or scaffolding to paint; he was too old to do a Michelangelo. Instead, the canvas and plastic panels were painted and then mounted on top of Lenepveu's original ceiling.

The tour moves on to the magnificent chandeliered halls for posing and pacing during the interval, the marbled bar, the gilt clocks and the Opéra museum, which includes sketches and paintings by Degas. Every niche contains a statue or a painting; no wonder designers use the foyers every year for fashion shows.

The building inspired Gaston Leroux's novel, *The Phantom of the Opera*, and the subsequent musical. For when work started on the building, excavators found an underground lake on the site, and spent some years pumping it out. Leroux's anti-hero, a mad engineer called Erik, was supposed to have built himself an underground palace at the other side of the lake.

But the true phantom is Garnier himself; one is constantly aware of his presence. Perhaps that's why they eventually did him down and placed his gilded statue (by the highly regarded Jean Baptiste Carpeaux) at the side entrance in the street.

1   PALAIS GARNIER, Place de l'Opéra, 9th, M Opéra, 01 44 73 13 04, 10am-4.30pm, F30.
2   French guided tours of the Opéra, 1pm daily (except Mon), Fr50. Paris Walking Tours conduct guided visits to the Opéra in English twice a month, 01 48 09 21 40, Fr60.

"I was mooching around for presents in Fauchon – the grandiose delicatessen which makes Fortnum and Mason look like a 7-Eleven – getting pleasantly stoned on the smell of coffee, when my reverie was interrupted by a small jar. 'Honey,' it said, 'collected on the roofs of the Opéra of Paris.' Surely some mistake, I thought. Our office looks out on the Opéra, surrounded by boulevards pullulating with pollution. If you leave the window open, your desk turns black. How could flowers, let alone bees, survive carbon-monoxide poisoning on a par with Mexico City? Out of journalistic duty, I bought the honey and made some inquiries. Fauchon assured me of the honey's safety, claiming bees were 'fine natural filters'. A few years ago, an apiarist called Jean Paucton asked a mate at the Opéra to store a couple of hives for him. They were dumped on the roof. Some months later, when M. Paucton arrived to take his hives to the country, both were occupied. Pinstriped bees were feeding off city flower boxes and the Tuileries. 'They swarm very rarely,' reassured Fauchon. In appearance, the honey is rather murky. On the palate, it is flowery and sweet. The aftertaste? Diesel.

METRO MUSIC

The dark underbelly

Going Underground: This report comes from the Métro, home at the lowest level to some of the highest artistic sensibility in France. I speak of the great and continuing work of Antoine Naso, the transport official who abolished penny buskers on the subway and replaced them with entire orchestras from the Paris Conservatoire.

Much as Paris parks ruthlessly pollard their trees each winter to ensure uniform beauty in summer, so Monsieur Naso weeds out the dross of the city's troglodite musical talent. Over 800 groups and individuals vie each autumn for M. Naso's 300 licences as official Métro musicians, with photo IDs. The criteria are strict, the auditions bloody, since musicians without their official name, rank and serial number can be summarily 'disappeared' by the Métro police.

M. Naso invites me to witness the selection. He operates from the seedy end of the Rue de Charonne, between a pen shop and a Salvation Army women's hostel. There's no one around but a high-pitched squealing comes from a spiral stairwell to the basement. Suddenly, I'm trapped in a tiny windowless room with eight South American peasants straight out of a coffee advert, playing

Andean pipes, dwarf guitars and *Bam-bo-ler-o!* – a Gipsy
King's favourite – at full volume. My instinct is to split, but
the lead singer rolls his eyes up to God and says, 'Mr Naso,
he upstairs.'

What a splendid figure M. Naso is, a truncated
Richard Gere with a fashionably short beard, a Gaultier-
type jacket and a red tie featuring paddle steamers. It's as
cutting edge as you get in urban transportation circles.

M. Naso's crusade began almost two years ago, in an
attempt to stamp out the hopeless and musically incompe-
tent 'who grate on people's ears'. His chosen buskers do
not hassle for money, merely laying a hat or box before
them, and they can't play on the train itself. 'People like
peace there to read their books,' he notes. It's all high
culture down under.

On his own books now, he has 40 classical students
from the Paris Conservatoire who rotate in an orchestra of
ten – 'they'd block the tunnels otherwise' – a Japanese harp
player, endless quartets, and some modern jazz ensembles.
'We also do weddings,' says M. Naso. Weddings? 'We
recommend particular groups to people, and often Métro
exposure leads to a CD. He videos every audition, a
subterranean A&R man.

We go down to judge the next group. Today's jury
includes a Métro security dude wearing an earring who
normally works on Line 2. He has a clipboard with the
name of the band and four boxes to tick: *Bon*, *Moyen*, *Passable*
and *Médiocre*. But what the bands are really watching is M.
Naso's trendily shod foot. Will it tap?

It remains understandably frozen during the performance of three minstrels, in full medieval get-up, equipped
with mandolins, curly shoes and plastic flowers in their hair.

I ask the lead singer to write down the group's name, which she does in indecipherable twirly medieval writing. Let's just translate it as 'The Jolly Troubadours'. 'What do you make an hour?' I ask. 'Fr100 each if we're lucky, but only in winter. In summer we're on the road doing medieval and New Age festivals.'

'That's nice,' I say. The guy from Line 2 tries to keep his face poker-straight.

A load of gourds and teak come down the stairs, followed by three Cameroonians. It's Bantou Sun, obviously one of M. Naso's favourites, for his toe taps and he offers them espresso afterwards. They are sure to get their licence renewed. It emerges the gourd-xylophone things are *balafons*, that Bantou Sun played specially for the Cameroon team in the World Cup, and that the best-paying stations are Châtelet, Montparnasse and Auber. 'You want a lot of *correspondances* [linking lines] so you get serious human traffic,' says the man with the biggest gourds.

Next comes the traditional long-haired busker with guitar, followed some minutes later by a man with a saxophone, intended for a separate audition. 'Hey!' they say to one another, 'long time no see. Let's jam.' So they do, and I think this is a fine way to spend a weekday afternoon.

The Métro, they say, is cheaper and warmer than a rehearsal room. The acoustics at Pigalle are particularly impressive, and there's a domed corner in Bastille Métro that's as good as a concert hall. 'You can tell if the stuff's good,' says the guitar, 'because the average passenger's got a 30-second attention span. If they stop, it's a big compliment.' No one actually lives by Métro playing alone. 'The worst thing is when people drop a coin in your box, and

then start taking change back,' says the sax. 'You have to
pretend you don't mind and just keep playing.'

I bid my farewells. 'I've got some new try-outs
coming in next week, some of whom will definitely fail,'
offers M. Naso hopefully. I ask who was the worst act ever.
'Well we had a transvestite. She not only played the key-
boards badly, and sang out of tune, but her stockings fell
down during the performance.' We can thank God and M.
Naso – who functions in much the same manner for the
underworld – that the ordinary commuter has been spared
this terrible sight.

❝When I first came to Paris aged ten, I was thrilled by
the unreliable vending machines in Métro stations that
sold tins of evil-smelling Parma violet comfits for a
franc. I was waiting recently on the platform at Opéra
when something odd attracted me to the new Selecta
vending machine. It was selling crisps, Kit-Kats,
Snickers, M&Ms, six-franc bags of madeleines and
Proust. Well, not quite Proust, but detective novels for
Fr10, the same price as a can of Coke. My particular
machine offered Gérard Delteil's *L'Or des Abbesses*, in
tribute to the Abbesses Métro station. It was 60 pages
of pulp fiction – perfect for an hour on a train – which
centred round a kidnapping in the Jardin des Plantes.
It turns out that stations all over Paris now sell the cult
'Metropolars' – subway-whodunits. The overground
RER train stations took to the idea first, but the
underground stations were particularly careful, insist-
ing that the murder mysteries should take place above
ground and off public transport, to avoid 'arousing

anxiousness or fear in the traveller'. So *Murder on the Orient Express* is out.

There are 18 titles, such as *Kill the Boss* and *The Dead Have a Hard Life* available from Editions de la Voûte. The publisher, Olivier Breton, says he sells around 3,000 of each novel, and the titles are changed weekly with the supplies of Twix.

      Ghosts trains are an evil necessity at Hallowe'en, but their year-round presence on the Paris Métro is well wicked. I speak of the new Météor line which moves in mysterious ways: fast, and without a driver.

Although there are passenger seats where the driver's should be, few adults dare sit before the giant windscreen as the train hurtles into the void.

Only children don't sense the taboo so it appears from the platform that trains are being driven by three-year-olds in Tintin anoraks. Then the doors open, and a disembodied voice barks orders in German. The French message gets lost in the barrage. But you can't get out because the train is sealed in stations in a giant Perspex tube, with doors that open precisely in line with the carriage doors.

'To prevent suicides and accidents,' says the Métro management, but it brings on havering claustrophobia instead. Who can say what may happen when the central computer catches a winter virus . . .

You might assume that the invisible-hand-style Métro would at least save on employment costs. Wrong. All the guards and drivers are being redeployed as 'greeters' or video spies. And you might cherish the hope that technology would end strikes.

Wrong again. The driverless railway at the airport was mysteriously immobilized for days by 'social unrest'.

The Météor line runs between the Madeleine (home of the Fauchon delicatessen) and the new Mitterrand library. Since Mitterrand's nickname was 'uncle' of 'Tonton', natives call it the Tonton-Fauchon line. It maybe no more functional than the rest of the Métro, but it is beautiful. The new hell-deep station at the Madeleine boasts a concourse filled with palm trees, each with its personal UV light for underground growth; pink, grey and cream granite floors; see-through escalators; great silver ceiling ducts filled with wires; display cases of modern art (purple plastic brain-chairs, and the like) and constant video surveillance. All in all, it worryingly resembles the high-tech HQ of every James Bond villain, just before the computer explodes and live cables torch everyone to death.

HAMMAM
AT THE MOSQUE
Tea, tiles, and Turkish baths

Cross the road from the Jardin des Plantes, go through the great arched doorway and you enter Marrakesh in the decadent 1920s. This is the Hammam de la Mosquée[1] where, deep in secret chambers tiled in green and gold and blue, bodies bask in clouds of steam. The silence is broken only by the trickle of water from a leafy fountain.

The experience cannot be compared to a sauna, or to one of those municipal Turkish baths in Britain with their sandpaper towels. The Hammam is luxurious, not ascetic, dedicated to hedonism rather than mere cleanliness.

The pleasure-seeker pays Fr85 to enter the labyrinth, which is structured rather like the interior of a pyramid with antechamber leading to antechamber until the heart – in this case the 90°C steam room – is reached.

The architecture is stunning. The largest room is cream marble with turquoise mosaic pillars. High up, arched windows let in shafts of sunlight above the steam. There are six alcoves with marble platforms, on each of which you can dimly make out two or three naked women in the mist, each a *tableau vivant* or something from a Seurat. Occasionally they move to douse themselves with cold water or unguents, but the norm is total languor.

Beyond this is the inner sanctum where only a few hardened women remain for any time, their eyes popping. But the stew is worth bearing to leap into the blue circular plunge pool, with the added pleasure of splashing the smug boiling ones with icy water and then apologizing profusely.

Afterwards, with pores pinging closed, you walk back weakly to the rest and massage room, lie back on the plastic-cushioned platforms and stare up at the gold, green and red-painted ceiling and the carved pillars. Surrounded by exquisite painted panels and prone women ranging from the beautiful to the enormous, there is a strong feeling of being in a harem. You keep expecting to see eunuchs.

The sound of the gentle slap of oil on flesh comes from the massage table – an extra Fr55 for ten minutes and well worth it. The masseuse, breaking the gargantuan stereotype, wears a neat white dress and a bun. Something called *gommage* is also offered, apparently a vicious rub-down with a loofah.

The rare conversations are not thrilling – perhaps on the men-only days shady business deals are done cloaked in steam. The ladies, all French, compare anti-cellulite creams, and there is detailed analysis of the latest make-up removers and face masks.

For the foreign voyeur, there is added interest in the French figure and the mysterious effect of tailoring upon it. Rather like Dr Who's Tardis with its inside larger than its outside, in the Hammam big slack-fleshed bodies emerge from perfectly cut little suits. The sight is cheering to the tourist who has been psychologically undermined by French feminine chic for days.

Final recuperation from city stress occurs outside in the mosque's Moorish courtyard, filled with roses, trees and café tables. For Fr10 there is sweet mint tea and waiters offer pastries of honey and dates. In a glass case there is rosewater and lemon Turkish delight the size of building blocks.

On leaving, the mosque can be visited from the Place du Puits-de-l'Ermite entrance at the back. There are green tiles, carved doors and pink marble fountains, and a guided tour if you ask. Ironically, the money for this compound dedicated to religion and pleasure came from the French in 1926, as a gesture of gratitude to the North Africans who fought in the First World War.

1   HAMMAM DE LA MOSQUEE, 39 Rue Geoffroy-St-Hilaire, 5th,
        M. Monge, 01 43 31 18 14. Women only: 10am-9pm Mon, Wed,
        Thurs, Fri, Sat. Men only: Tues afternoon and Sun. Bring towels.
Other baths: Les Bains d'Odessa, 5 Rue Odessa, 14th, M Montparnasse,
    01 43 20 91 21. Cleopatra Club, 53 Boulevard de Belleville, 11th,
    M Couronnes, 01 43 57 34 32. Women only.

66France is in mourning for the bidet. According to
    Jacob Defalon, the Armitage Shanks equivalent, only
    one in ten Gallic bathrooms now boasts a bidet, and it
has been ousted by the shower. Which leads us to ask:
what was a bidet for precisely? Why does the word
bidet come from the French for 'old nag'? Why was
the bidet suddenly found to be necessary in
Napoleonic times, when people had coped perfectly
well without it before?

In writing obituaries of the bidet, some writers
have excelled themselves. Gaella Guernalec in *France-*

Soir felt that 'bidet' was too base a name for such a worldly object: 'When this typically French invention was nicknamed 'the ladies' confidante', it was blessed with implicit poetry. When the husband rolled over afterwards to fall asleep, having forgotten to say 'I love you', the bidet watched as the wife's tears of sadness flowed.

PARIS
AFTER DARK

NIGHTLIFE

Don't show up before tomorrow

There are untold *faux pas* just waiting to be made in the sub-terranean world of the Paris nightclub. For a start, nightlife does not begin until the early morning – showing up at a club before 1am is seen as gauche or desperate. Then there is the struggle to cross the threshold-of-the-moment, often denied if you are not on some secret guest list or one of *les lookés* – the trendy and beautiful.

It is too risky to predict the popularity of particular clubs, but trends include the continuing rise of salsa, tango and samba nights as well as world parties; the appearance of small late-drinking clubs and restaurants; and the disco revival.

Dedicated clubbers weigh their options seriously, consulting the monthly *Nova* magazine, and its listings section detailing specific nights at each club, one-off raves and events, prices and addresses. Some clubs let women or *les nanas* in free at the start of the night, in order to lure *les mecs* – the guys. This is helpful, since most clubs charge F60 to F140, and drinks are astronomical. For daily club news, tune into Radio Nova on 101.5MHz at 6pm. In Figaroscope in Wednesday's *Figaro* newspaper, there is a 'Nocturne' listing of clubs and parties. Otherwise, the Time Out English section of *Pariscope* magazine provides a limited guide.

The old-fashioned 1936 dancehall Le Balajo[1] has regained prominence with its Latino nights, as has La Java[2] in Belleville, but be warned that French clubbers tend to take lessons in salsa or tango and display their expertise. Nothing more embarrassing than being whisked off by a snake-hipped Frenchman, only to lumber pathetically in his arms. The serious attention paid to dancing means that the Latino clubs are not forced into becoming a meat market. The Java also used to be a dancehall, featuring Edith Piaf, and it still has tea dances at the weekends.

Also in the increasingly happening Belleville – Menilmontant area is La Flèche d'Or[3], an old railway station converted into a bar with mismatched tables and an equally mismatched clientele. It is more scruffy than glitzy, but incredibly right-on, with bands and dancing at the weekends.

The true disco experience can still be had at Queen[4], a large gay club which has mixed nights including Saturday. Platform boots and glitter may be worn for disco, although there are also more mainstream techno-house nights. Sadly, Les Mousses, summer nights during which the dancefloor is sprayed waist-high with foam, are men only.

Les Bains[5] is Eurotrash heaven, with rich men in suits and supermodels dancing in the former Turkish baths. Ordinary human beings consider themselves lucky to be able to pay the large admission – the doorperson is Marilyn, an enormous woman with unfathomable tastes. Unless you have access to the VIP enclosure or wear the full Prada uniform, expect difficulties.

For those whose needs extend merely to dancing and having a good time without draconian door policies, the twice-monthly Bal[6] on Saturdays at the Elysée Montmartre is a good bet. The 12-piece Golam big band play cover versions of everything from the Sex Pistols to Rap and French pop, and dancing varies from club-style to *bal-musette* waltzing.

Both the Métro and the limited evening bus service stop just after midnight. Night buses run every hour on a few routes, but most people take taxis. At popular late-night places such as Châtelet and the Bastille, there is often a long wait at ranks, making it worthwhile to walk or call a taxi before you leave the club.

For those tired by even this talk of late nights and dancing expertise, there are the afternoon tea dances at La Coupole[7] in Montparnasse, friendly events featuring all ages, starting at 3pm on Saturdays and Sundays with a bizarre mix of tango, disco and Latino. You can sit out at tables and calmly drink cocktails – or, indeed, tea – without feeling pressured to dance. On Tuesday nights, from 9pm (which means after 11pm really) until 3am, there is a Latino night on the small basement dancefloor, among the pillars and art deco decor. It's a cross between *Come Dancing* and being in Rio, as expert salsa dancers show off their skill and flesh in extraordinary satin ensembles. Here, strangers versed in Latino intricacies will ask you to dance – in a clinch – but making mistakes is the only way to learn, and people are very tolerant. The music is provided by an authentic band, and in between, a DJ. *Aficionados* drink copious water and buy a bottle of rum for their table, which lasts all night.

Life starts in jazz clubs before midnight too, and there's never the clothes question. You should be guided by your favourite sort of music (again, *Pariscope*), but you can always be sure to find something decent from 11pm at the

All Jazz Club[8] in the heart of St Germain, or from 9pm at
New Morning[9] on the Right Bank.

1   LE BALAJO, 9 Rue de Lappe, 11th, M Bastille, 01 47 00 07 87.
2   LA JAVA, 105 Rue Faubourg du Temple, 11th, M Belleville,
     01 42 02 20 52.
3   LA FLECHE D'OR, 102bis Rue de Bagnolet, 20th,
     M Alexandre Dumas, 01 43 72 04 23.
4   QUEEN, 102 Avenue des Champs-Elysées, 8th, M George V,
     01 42 89 31 32.
5   LES BAINS, 7 Rue du Bourg-l'Abbé, 3rd, M Etienne-Marcel,
     01 48 87 01 80.
6   LE BAL, Elysée Montmartre, 72 Boulevard Rochechouart, 18th,
     M Anvers, 01 44 92 45 42.
7   LA COUPOLE, 102 Boulevard de Montparnasse, 15th, M Vavin,
     01 43 20 14 20.
8   ALL JAZZ CLUB, 7 Rue St-Benoît, 6th, M St Germain,
     01 42 61 87 02.
9   NEW MORNING, 7 Rue des Petites Ecuries, 10th, M Château-d'Eau,
     01 45 23 51 41.

GAY PAREE

Legacy of Oscar and Gertrude

Eccentrics and gays have always come to Paris to get away from their parents, or their nation. No other city had the tolerance to house men, from André Gide to James Baldwin, and women from Colette to Gertrude Stein.

It was Sylvia Beach, the gay proprietress of Shakespeare and Co on the Left Bank, who published the first edition of Joyce's *Ulysses* in 1922. Oscar Wilde came here to spend the last years of his life in an atmosphere less stuffy than that of England. James Baldwin, the black American writer, was here in the 1950s for the city's sexual and racial freedom.

Although their purposes were primarily literary, many great gay writers, French and foreign, were also here for the good time. Gide was a wildly liberating force; Jean Genet's misbehaviour was legendary. As the normally conservative *Figaro* newspaper put it the other day: 'Genet elevated the coarse to some kind of chivalry, and made being a pariah poetic.'

Paris is full of shrines to those poetic pariahs. There are official sites, such as Marcel Proust's cork-lined study on the Boulevard Haussmann, and unofficial sites, which include most of the once-seedy hotels on the Left Bank, which at some point housed every gay typist in town. One can also wander by the apartment at 27 Rue de Fleurus where Alice B. Toklas cooked for Stein and Picasso, and go over to Père Lachaise cemetery to visit Oscar Wilde, his grave topped with a boy angel, now left with a stump after neutering by an offended cemetery worker.

These writers would probably have had a low opinion of anything as institutionalized as Gay Pride week, but Gay Paree has changed, and such events are an integral part of gay and lesbian life here. The city fills up with visitors for the Gay Pride march every June, always a spectacle, involving men in wedding dresses on rollerblades and the traditional dykes on bikes.

Meanwhile, clubs such as Queen[1] have organized special nights, all of which can be checked out in the useful Time Out English section in the French listings' magazine, *Pariscope*. Gay nightlife is ever-changing, so check venues weekly. But the most traditional taste of gay Paris can be found at the Sunday afternoon tea dances.

Simone de Beauvoir used to take her young girl-friends (in both senses) to tea dances, where they would dance away the afternoons with men, women and each other. Nowadays, the main heterosexual tea dance is at La Coupole in Montparnasse, but the men-only dances at La Locomotive[2] are said to be extraordinary.

Afternoon tea dances are the only place, according to *aficionados*, where you see businessmen, couturiers, television presenters, bodybuilders and dancers together.

Dances begin at La Locomotive at 5pm on Sunday to DJs spinning something which is described as 'camp house' in the main room, while the basement 'Chaufferie' has, among other useful items, a bed. There's always time for confession afterwards.

Pulp[3] has similar tea dances for women, for those nostalgic for the days when girls wore lipstick and monocles and Les Scandaleuses is a great lesbian bar.

The gay literary scene is not what it was, but there is a good bookshop, Les Mots à la Bouche[4], at 6 Rue St Croix de la Brétonnerie on the main gay drag in the Marais. The hot book to read is a history of the French gay movement since 1968 called *Le Rose et Le Noir* by Frérdéric Martel. The pink is for gay emancipation, and the black for mourning in the age of Aids.

It was only in 1981 that French Secret Service files on homosexuals were destroyed and the legal age for homosexual activity reduced to 16. There is still some official reluctance to embrace the gay community which has taken over much of the Marais. Strolling the Rue Vieille du Temple and Rue St Croix de la Brétonnerie is like being suddenly deposited in San Francisco's Castro, but here the police will shut a club or bar at the very whiff of 'disturbance of the peace', and there have been complaints about the rainbow flags which signify gay or lesbian businesses.

Towards Châtelet there is the amusing Banana Café[5], with a mixed crowd and its Maître d'iresplendent, rotund and probably female in a rubber catsuit, high heels and Dame Edna *diamanté* spectacles.

For those who prefer the outdoor life, the great cruise zone is the Tuileries quai and esplanade above the Seine, on the Right Bank opposite the Musée d'Orsay. Many tourists are puzzled to see so many men sunbathing barechested there even on cold days. Now you know why.

1 QUEEN, 102 Avenue des Champs Elysées, 8th, M George V,
   01 42 89 31 32.

2 LA LOCOMOTIVE, 90 Boulevard de Clichy, 18th, M Place de Clichy,
   01 53 41 88 88.

3 PULP, 26 Boulevard Poissonière, 2nd, M Rue Montmartre,
   01 40 26 01 93.

4 LES MOTS À LA BOUCHE, 6 Rue St Croix de la Brétonnerie, 4th,
   M Hôtel-de-Ville, 01 42 78 88 30.

5 BANANA CAFÉ, 13 Rue de la Ferronnerie, 1st, M Châtelet-Les
   Halles, 01 42 33 35 31.

6 LES SCANDALEUSES, 8 Rue des Ecouffes, 4th, M Hôtel-de-Ville,
   01 48 87 39 26.

7 CENTRE GAI ET LESBIENNE, 3 Rue Keller; 11th, M Ledru-Rollin,
   01 43 57 21 47.

LE LOUNGING

Supper and Sofas

The once relaxing weekend abroad has become a cruel instrument of enrichment and erudition. I know this because we secretly give guests a culture count when they appropriate the Eurostar Memorial Sofabed in the Rue du Bac. The highest rating so far was earned by two academic types who, in 48 hours, saw a one-woman show inspired by the works of Simone de Beauvoir, the Musée D'Orsay (but not the Impressionists: 'dishtowel art', they said), the Jeu de Pomme, a matinée of the latest Peter Brooke play and a three-hour Serbian film which was unlikely to grace uncultured London. They also deposited a cheap houseplant on the grave of Russian writer Zamyatin and had dinner in one of the oldest bistros by the Bastille. For this, they scored the maximum ten points.

Imagine then, the delight at discovering what Parisians themselves do in London: 'I recently took a return trip on the Eurostar,' says a reader in the hip *Nova* listings magazine. 'I spent the day in bed there with a friend watching British television and eating pizzas.'

This kind of passive resistance, this valuing of consummation over cultural consumption, can only be admired. Why should there be an imperative to achieve while on holiday? I am not necessarily suggesting that visitors to Paris should remain in their hotels ordering room service – this is only possible in the very early stages of a relationship – but there is a lot to be said for lounging around doing next to nothing. Besides, Paris has the splendid A La Carte gourmet home delivery service[6], which lets you order dishes from the menus of 20 restaurants, from traditional French to Indian and sushi. Plus there is a champagne and caviar delivery, or croissants in the morning, if dressing to go to the *boulangerie* does not appeal.

Much lounging inspiration has come from Britain, particularly the clubs of Soho where Londoners drape themselves on sofas to a background of Easy Listening. Similar establishments have opened in Paris – Le Lounge Club du Zebra Square[1], Le Lizard Lounge[2] and Le Café de la Musique[3] have raised 'le lounging' the height of chic.

Lounging, it must be noted, is different from that early 1990s concept cocooning, where people stayed at home nesting a great deal. Lounging is the lazy version of café society – it must be done in public with good friends and as little mental effort as possible. Conversation must be relaxed. Arguments and over-enthusiastic debates are frowned upon. Philosophy is out.

Le Lounge Club is the finest example of the genre in Paris. The long smoking-room cum lounge is painted midnight blue, with enormous leather Chesterfields and armchairs on a wooden floor. Its murky interior suits those conducting illegitimate affairs, since you can barely see further than the bottom of 'le long drink', as they say here. Cocktails are much favoured and there is often a pianist playing, or CDs of Frank Sinatra, Paul Anka, Nat King Cole and cheesy Europop from the 1950s. The owner, Patrick Derdérian says he wanted to create *une ambiance musicale très crooner*. The Lizard Lounge in the Marais is less lethargic, and does a good brunch with British newspapers upstairs on Sundays.

The sharp, modern Café de la Musique is perhaps not worth the trip to the 19th alone, but if you plan to attend a concert at the Cité de la Musique complex, it gets you in that relaxed musaky mood beforehand. The fashionable habit of lounging has also caused a comeback for the glorious bar of the Hotel Lutétia[4] on the Left Bank. The womblike room is panelled with mahogany in the style of a grand ocean liner, with an art deco painting of the *Lutetia* cruise ship. The Margueritas, Kirs and Martinis are correctly executed and the chairs are comfortable. The hotel itself is a time warp – it harboured the Gestapo during the war, and was liberated by the Americans, among them Hemingway, and then housed refugees. Now it is lounge central. The Lutetia is also within strolling distance of the Bon Marché department store and Prada on the Rue de Grenelle for those who wish to slob and shop. The Hemingway bar at the Ritz and the Crillon Hotel bar are also eminently and expensively loungeable.

The newest *decontracté* – relaxed – spot is the upstairs bar at Terence Conran's London clone, the Alcazar[5] restaurant in St Germain. There are banquettes with fat velvet cushions, a grand piano when needed, and convenient people-watching over the restaurant below. It is uplifting to realize that Parisians recently learned the art of slobbing around from Britian, just as the British learn about culture

from France. This is one of the few successful exchange
mechanisms in the European Community so far.

1   LOUNGE CLUB DU ZEBRA SQUARE, 1 Rue de Boulainvilliers,
     16th, M La Muette, 01 44 14 91 90 (closed Sun, Mon evenings).
2   LE LIZARD LOUNGE, 18 Rue du Bourg-Tiebourg, 4th, M Hôtel de
     Ville, 01 42 72 81 34.
3   LE CAFÉ DE LA MUSIQUE, 213 Ave Jean-Jaurès, 19th, M Porte de
     Pantin, 01 48 03 15 91.
4   LUTETIA HOTEL BAR, Rue de Sèvres at Babylone, 6th, M Sèvres-
     Babylone, 01 49 54 46 46.
5   ALCAZAR, 62 Rue Mazarine, 6th, M St Germain, 01 53 10 19 99.
6   A La Carte gourmet home delivery: 01 45 00 12 12.

❝It was inevitable, given the variety in quality and
unexpected horrors and pleasures of the Paris
bathroom scene, that someone should see fit to provide
a Michelin-style guide to the subject. Titled *Gogues en
Vogue* – Fashionable Loos – the guide brings serious
analysis to a much-neglected subject. Instead of
Michelin stars, it awards a bleach symbol for cleanliness
and an air-freshener symbol for olfactory performance.

The truly sumptuous loos of Paris are in hotels such
as the Crillon (three bleaches, three air-fresheners):
'Not to be missed. The Ladies are particularly refined.
One enters a clean haven; three spacious cubicles
equipped with antique accessories, elegant lighting and
a marble floor . . . Majestic washbasins with gold taps
awaiting the touch of your manicured hands; an
immense and flattering mirror, space to redo your
make-up; and delightful Kleenex dispensers.'

Meanwhile, the Café Montecristo on the Champs-
Elysées is voted the worst (one bleach, one air-

freshener): 'Doors to Ladies and Gents indistinguish-
able because signs have been ripped off. Graffiti, marbled Formica, broken taps . . . the hygiene is dubious.
A tenacious odour, which cannot quite be pinned
down.'

CHILDREN'S
PARIS

ALLONS ENFANTS

Limiting parent pain

Recently, a family with three children arrived to stay at our apartment after a day of sightseeing in the city. The kids were exhausted, but still rabid from the Es in the ice-cream and chocolate consumed all day. By the time we'd put them to bed in their new Paris T-shirts in sleeping bags on the floor and a portacot, it was already 9pm. Immediately, the husband collapsed into a deep sleep and the wife burst into tears.

To avoid this happening to you, military precision is required in planning the day, particularly in bad weather. In fact, child-friendly places abound in Paris, because the city is full of native children without gardens or much indoor space. Certain restaurants, such as the Hippopotamus chain, are utterly child friendly; most cafés are helpful; and small children are acceptable at lunchtime in most bistros and brasseries, although they are less welcome in the evening. At night, consider regaining your sanity by abandoning your children with an English-speaking baby-sitter, who can be booked on the day and will come to hotels or apartments. The agency Kid Service[1] generally uses students as babysitters, and you can specify a bilingual woman when you call.

Families can easily tackle the traditional sites like the Eiffel Tower, but suggest your children do it in the early evening when there are no long queues of other people's whining offspring, and the view is more spectacular. Children may also now demand Notre Dame Cathedral following the success of the Hunchback cartoon, but be warned that tourist levels are at such a height it has been renamed Notre Disney by the locals. There are 273 winding stone steps up to the gargoyles on the towers, but if some of your family are too small or stiff to make it, there is a pleasant children's sandpit and benches round the back of the cathedral. A boat trip on the Seine which passes the cathedral is perhaps a less painful experience.

A visit to a park is essential, since you can sit still in a tree-shaded café while they run around screaming. The Jardin des Tuileries is central, but the children's playpark is fairly small. There are, however, pony rides and a traditional old roundabout or *manège* with painted horses and elephants. In the summer, an enormous funfair with a big wheel sets up in the Tuileries. There is that staple of every French childhood memory, the boating pond, where wooden toy yachts can be rented for a few francs, and pushed off with sticks. Café life in the park is varied, with delicious fruit tarts at Café Véry.

You cannot go wrong with the Jardin du Luxembourg, whatever age the child. There is a special fenced playground for the under-sixes near the Orangerie. It has potted palm trees, four sandpits, two paddling pools in summer and plenty of benches. Later, you can take them to see the four o'clock performance of the *Guignols*, a Punch and Judy-style show. For older children, a fee of F8 gives entry to the best adventure playground in Paris. It is sectioned by age, with little rocking animals and wooden cars and trains as well as a sandpit for toddlers, and more dangerous-looking triangular climbing frames and rope swings for older children. Best of all, the playground hut dispenses coffee and snacks, and there are bathrooms (a rarity here).

French television personalities and a smattering of actresses bring their children for Saturday or Sunday lunch outdoors (even in autumn and spring) to the Luxembourg café by the *Guignols* and the roundabout. There is a sympathetic welcome, and changing *plats du jour* and *crêpes*. All the local children eat sliced ham with sautéd, cubed potatoes and drink grenadine.

Another of our favourites is the Musée Rodin, which has exquisite formal gardens behind the private mansion which now houses the sculpture. Mothers of France – i.e. anyone with young children or a pram – get in free to the garden, which is full of Rodin sculptures, including the *Burghers of Calais* and *The Thinker*. Even small children seem to love the statues, and there are two sandpits at the end of the garden when interest wanes. The café opens most of the year, for children are nicer when they're kept fuelled.

If you have a car or taxi, the Bois de Boulogne is only 15 minutes from the centre of Paris. The woods are perfect for older children – boats, horses, and bicycles can be rented by the hour – and there is the Jardin d'Acclimatation[2] for the younger ones, which can also be reached by miniature train from Porte Maillot Métro. A strange combination of a zoo, funfair and green picnic spot, the Jardin costs a mere Fr10 for hours of entertainment. There is a mini-farm, with shiny pink pigs, goats, sheep, donkeys and hens. There is a partial zoo, with brown bears, monkeys and deer, and there are rides suitable for small children. Another miniature railway goes round the entire park, and on certain days – call ahead – there are workshops for children. If it rains, there is an indoor playhouse with rooms filled with foam shapes and bouncy balls, and you can leave your children there, supervised for up to two hours while you dine in some pleasant restaurant in the Bois.

There are two solutions to the museum problem. One is to aim for a small child's naptime, but be warned that the stairs of the Louvre[3] and the Musée d'Orsay could be more pram-friendly. If you have older children, there are daily painting and design workshops in the summer at the Louvre and the Pompidou Centre[3]. Even though they are in French, much of the work is practical – making small models, drawings or paintings – and they usually include a short tour of one aspect of the collection. The parents can then sneak off for an hour and a half of uninterrupted viewing.

The Jardin des Plantes[4] is my ideal spot when you're not sure of the weather. There's the rather scroggy but enjoyable Ménagerie, or zoo outdoors, and the Jardin's Natural History museum and Paleontology (dinosaur section) if it rains. The museum is an enormous, ancient building, but the collection of stuffed animals is modernized with great displays, light-and-sound jungle and savannah sounds, and touch-screen computers. Children can run and shout, and no one will pay them the slightest attention. The animals are not in cases, but standing on the floor, with a foot-high fence around them. It's as close as you'll ever get to a giraffe or an anaconda. The café does great *gaufres* – hot sugar waffles – and is on a glass balcony overlooking a giant whale skeleton.

More *ringard* – cheesily out-dated – is the Musée de

l'Homme, with lots of Eskimos, American Indian tepees, apemen, miniature Turkish bazaars and African carvings. Although it's all a bit dusty, children love it. The museum is in the Palais de Chaillot and its Totem restaurant looks over the river to the Eiffel Tower.

1   KID SERVICE, 01 42 61 90 00, bilingual babysitting at Fr33 an hour, plus Fr60 agency fee.
2   JARDIN D'ACCLIMATATION, Bois de Bologne, 16th, 01 40 67 90 80.
3   ATELIERS (workshops) POUR ENFANTS: Louvre, M Louvre-Rivoli for children 6 to 13, 2.15pm daily in summer, F28, reservations 01 40 20 52 63. Pompidou Centre, design workshop for children 6–12, 2.30pm daily in summer, Wednesday and Saturday in termtime, F30 (includes adult ticket), M Hôtel de Ville, 01 44 78 12 33.
4   JARDIN DES PLANTES MÉNAGERIE and MUSÉE D'HISTORE NATURELLE (shut Tues), 57 Rue Cuvier, 5th, M Jussieu, 01 40 79 30 00.
5   MUSÉE DE L'HOMME (shut Tues), Palais de Chaillot, Place du Trocadéro, 16th, M Trocédéro, 01 44 05 72 72.

❝Colonialism is alive and well in the heart of Paris: on the Enchanted River ride in the celebrated children's park, Le Jardin d'Acclimatation. Unsuspecting, we took our children on one of the rickety boats that trundle slowly along the Enchanted River – basically a large ditch. Suddenly, out of the undergrowth loomed a coffee-coloured man in a pith helmet and a white linen suit. Seconds later, round another bend, was a painted black colonial administrator in an old school tie, followed by another shiny native in a vest happily picking cotton or coffee. 'Wassat?' said my younger son. 'Lotsa mans!'

Lotsa politically incorrect mans, really, but how do you explain that to a one-year-old? The Enchanted

River ride was created in 1952, as France was pulling
out of colonies all over the world and suffering from
dodgy nostalgia. Although the entire park is being
updated, the Enchanted River will be left untouched.
There is no question of changing 'the naïve and
humorous wooden statues from the Ivory Coast', said
the PR, a little edgily.

"We've got the video, read the picture book, so we
decided to visit the real thing: the hunchback of Notre
Dame. My three-year-old son was delighted when
informed of our destination. 'We're going to see
Quasimodo?' he inquired in his best Disney – Victor
Hugo doesn't get a look in nowadays. I said I couldn't
guarantee anything, but I suspected Quasimodo was no
longer with us. Unperturbed, my son started running
up the 273 stone steps to the towers. For someone
who can become mysteriously fatigued and in need of
a piggy back and smelling salts on the shortest trip to
the supermarket, this was an extraordinary physical
feat. (An American study made basketball champions
copy toddlers for a day, jumping off giant chairs,
throwing tantrums, climbing stairs each half their
height. The basketballers threw in the towel at midday,
while the toddlers went on and on and on.)

I panted behind my son as we reached the viewing
platform. 'Tigers! Dragons!' he shouted, paralytic with
excitement at the gargoyles. 'Where's Quasimodo?'
I made some pretence of looking around for the hunchback, which was a mistake. My child started doing his
Quasimodo imitation, normally performed naked after
a bath, with bow legs, hunched shoulders and dangling

arms. How he's picked this up, I don't know, because the Disney book, in a miracle of political correctness, does not mention the word hunchback. An ugly tourist passed us in an enormous green puffa jacket, which made him look like an American footballer or . . . 'Quasimodo!' shouted my son. 'There's Quasimodo!' and pursued his victim into the bell tower.

On a damp winter Sunday, as striking lorry drivers tightened their blockade of Parisian stomachs and politicians (as they do with unfailing regularity every year), we went for a walk in the Jardin des Plantes. Water dripped from broken windows in the cast-iron greenhouses, bedraggled with rust. The place was deserted, half the buildings shut, and the only sound as the sky darkened at 3pm was the creak of the pram wheels. The ancient zoo there qualified for a Gothic horror film. Flabby, bow-legged lions paced cages designed when Africa was still the Dark Continent, and a brown bear begged half-heartedly for biscuits in a stone pit.

We were transported to another time, 1870 to be precise, when Paris was under siege from Prussians rather than *routiers*. Then, food supplies ran so short after four months that citizens who tired of rat and cat fricassees turned to the zoo for sustenance. Victor Hugo was sent joints of bear, deer and antelope by the Jardin des Plantes. Kangaroo was consumed at the fashionable Chez Brébant restaurant, and wolf steaks graced the best butcher in Faubourg St Honoré. The hippo survived because it failed to meet the reserve price of Fr80,000, but Castor and Pollux, two young elephants, went straight in the pot, including their trunks. One Englishman abroad noted. 'I have now dined off camel, antelope, dog, donkey, mule and elephant, which I approve of in the order in which I have written.'

Was it then merely a coincidence that a fashion for exotic meats appeared to grip Paris just as the lorry stranglehold tightened? Were those rusting old cages being pillaged by enterprising restaurateurs at night? The Lutetia Brasserie on the Left Bank started serving ostrich, and suddenly food inspectors at last allowed kangaroo meat to appear on the menu of Wooloomooloo, the city's gourmet Australian restaurant, (36 Boulevard Henri IV, 4th, M. Bastille, 01 42 72 32 11). I took the husband there one evening as my official taster for the kangaroo steak.

'Can't hang it by law here, so it doesn't taste very gamey,' said the waiter helpfully. 'It is, of course, free-range kangaroo.' The 'roo arrived rare, in long, thick strips. Tail? I wondered, but said nothing. It languished in a pool of bloody gravy. 'Well, they've been quite daring, really, letting the kangaroo taste come through and not smothering it in some thick sauce,' said the husband chewing bravely. 'First marsupial I've ever eaten.'

The husband is no virgin on the exotic meat front – he has eaten alligator, rattlesnake, python and ostrich. He rated the 'roo below ostrich but above python, and finished the entire plate. It was later, at a party, that he began to look uncomfortable. The 'roo was not as digestible as it appeared. 'How do you feel?' I whispered. 'A bit jumpy,' he said.

CLOTHES
– AND MANNERS –
FOR KIDS

Looking Parisian for less

In the heart of the 7th *arrondissement*, the Kensington and Chelsea of Paris, a child is born. Maman and papa already know his sex, in order that from his first cry he can be wrapped in the appropriate colours. His parents lay him in a Silver Cross pram, and wise men, ladies-who-lunch and business associates arrive bearing gifts from the *liste de naissance* lodged at Bonpoint.

The child can barely focus on his Barbar mobile, but already his preferences are being carefully formed. While in the womb he became a treasured customer at Bonpoint, perhaps the poshest baby emporium on earth, and situated conveniently in the 7th. There, his parents relieved themselves of a minimum of £2,000 to buy his basic layette. He is dressed in pale blue pyjama-suits with white smocking, on which, mysteriously, he never, ever dribbles.

The life of Edouard, Charles, Henri, Gaspard or Stanislas – only certain traditional names are deemed appropriate among the upper classes – will continue for ever as it began, in the best possible taste.

Watch perfectly dressed French children, and you can learn a great deal about the nation. Being a blank slate, an object that can for some years be outfitted, controlled and paraded, the French child becomes mini-distillation of its parents' desires. Among the *haute bourgeoisie*, there is whole slew of traditions and dress codes which are violated on pain of excommunication. If the Paris maman never leaves the house looking creased and scruffy, then neither shall her child.

It is fortunate that the French Government gives increasing tax allowances with each child, because remaining BCBG (bon chic bon genre) is by no means cheap – buying the traditional woollen blazer (dry clean only) with contrasting piping every year costs £60, and only one Swiss make suffices. The essential smocked party dress from Baby Dior or Bonpoint might set you back £180, and as for the import prices on Start-Rite shoes . . .

Marie-France Cohen says she set up Bonpoint nearly 30 years ago 'to provide classic clothes which are fashionable, but not a vulgar imitation of adult fashions'. Her customers include the Duchess of York who buys those frilly matching dresses and socks for Beatrice and Eugénie and somehow makes them look like they came from Tesco. Bonpoint's French customers are the usual bunch of Rothschilds and Vuittons, as well as Princess Caroline of Monaco, Isabelle Adjani and Martin Chirac, the grandson of the president. Mme Cohen has 30 shops around the world including two in London and notes caustically that the highest spenders are not necessarily the fastest bill payers.

The cross-Channel snobbery is revealing – the French want English prams, shoes and Norland nannies, while the English buy French clothes. Evelyne Vandenbroucque, who runs International Nannies in Paris, says: 'Eighty per cent of my French customers come to me for English nannies. There

is no nanny training system here, so they often want girls
trained by Norland or Chiltern.'

There may be a demand for British nannies here, but
there is no call for Mothercare economy 3-packs of sleep-
suits. Such a utilitarian thought horrifies Mme Cohen. 'The
more you go south in Europe, the more people spend on
their children,' she dictates. 'The Italians spend a lot, but go
north into more Protestant countries like England and
Scotland and they get meaner.'

It only took a few days, never mind years, as a Scot
living in France with my two small sons, to realize we
would never make the social and sartorial grade in the
Jardin du Luxembourg. On Sundays, after an enormous
family lunch, Parisians parade their children there in outfits
the British would reserve for weddings and funerals. In
summer there are sailor suits, in winter wool coats with
velvet collars and shoes designed for dancing, not playing.
By contrast, my children dress, mostly from kind donations
and the Baby Gap sale, like rappers just released from
prison. Often they behave like that too. For some time my
elder son would not leave home without a blue baseball cap
saying illiterately 'Toys Factory', and my younger without a
pair of red plastic cowboy boots.

When ladies in Paris shops pat my son's head and say:
'*Est-il sage?*' which means is he well behaved, docile? – a
great compliment here – I am forced to smile mendacious-
ly. For French children not only dress well and remain clean
all day, but have impeccable manners too. You never see
them on supermarket floors having a tantrum. There is firm
discipline in the home which results in docile behaviour
outside. A French friend has a theory that her country-
women only smack their children between the ages of 12

and 18 months, when verbal reasoning is useless, and there-after the kids stay in line.

Discipline and manners are major preoccupations of Laurence Pernoud, author of the classic French text *Raising My Child*, and a terrifying combination of Lady Thatcher and Dr Spock. None of your Penelope Leach permissiveness here – there is a whole chapter on 'Silent Education' which deals with 'paternal discipline, authority, overprotection and aggressiveness'. 'Children become more and more insolent to see how far they can go. Authority is necessary to keep them balanced . . . thus bit by bit the child learns to master his emotions.'

Although France is a country which loves children, it is not child-centric. Children are never allowed to become tyrants, but must fit in with their parents' lives. I remember talking at dinner to an Enarque – a graduate of France's grand civil service school – about my children's night wakenings and he said: 'I am firmly of the view that if the parents are happy, the baby is happy, so I suggest you shut the door. Perhaps even two doors.' (He was right.)

Parental convenience is all, not merely nowadays with the wonderful nursery and pre-school systems in France, but in the past. In 1840, Louise Colet, who eventu-ally became Flaubert's mistress and the model for Madame Bovary, sent her baby daughter for two years to the finest wet nurse in Nanterre, a village outside Paris. The upper classes of Paris believed the city air was bad for a child. The upper classes of Paris also continued partying and never suffered a sleepness night.

Even now, no self-respecting Parisian maman suffers much sleeplessness. Women's magazines are full of reassur-ing suggestions that breastfeeding for even two weeks is helpful, a month is heroic, and three months is really beyond the call of duty. Another French friend said: 'After six weeks I couldn't stand it, so I gave up, added cereal to his last bottle, as the doctor recommended, and let him cry until he slept through the night. It was too much for me otherwise. I look terrible without sleep.' Besides, leaky breasts are really not very chic. Neither is a sagging stomach, but fortunately, the French Government can help. The state actually pays for ten post-natal therapy sessions to ensure women remain tight-muscled and flat stomached. 'It was like having a free personal trainer,' said a delighted English mother in Paris.

Appearances, whether of parent or child, matter more here. The well-dressed child is more than an accessory – it is a statement about the social and financial worth of the family. Parisians, particularly, may live in small apartments but are famous for 'wearing their money on their backs'. Drawing the line at actually pinning large denomination notes on my younger son to improve his social acceptability, I decided to try to disguise him as a French child. We went shopping.

We rolled up in the pushchair to Tartine et Chocolat, at the grander end of Boulevard St Germain. My son pointed excitedly to a beige linen safari suit with bone buttons. Smart, I thought, not overstated, and he can iron it himself. We inquired after the price: £100. We regrouped. Perhaps, I said, if you cannot look like a French child, you can smell like one. My son agreed to be the 'nose' for the baby perfumes (one cannot say aftershaves), without which no self-respecting French child leaves home, and we went off to sample each fragrance in the corresponding shop.

Our first experiment was with Jacadi's L'Eau des

Grands at Fr140. I sprayed a generous amount of the strong, flowery, fruity stuff on my wrist. I held it close to my child's nose. He recoiled deep into his pushchair and made the face he makes when rejecting spinach.

Tartine et Chocolat's Ptisenbon – a shortening of 'little one smells nice' – went down little better. My son then tried to eat the Ptisenbon lip balm, which came in a pale blue lipstick-style tube. We were too embarrassed to talk prices and left.

At Bonpoint, we looked into purchasing a navy-blue jacket with gold buttons, the sort of thing French babies probably wear to the golf club, but the £140 price tag held us back. We inquired after scents instead and were offered a marvellous pong for F260, made for Bonpoint by the chi-chi Annick Goutal. I felt it was a 1990s scent, a little like the unisex CK1, without being too heavy. My son made no comment. Then he began to whimper with boredom.

Although all the saleswomen assured us the scents were *mixte*, I was not convinced. Perhaps a Scots boy was too rough and ready for the 'nose' experience, lacking in sensitivity. I confided my worries to a French girlfriend who has a beautiful daughter of 16 months. She said little girls react with far more interest. 'I spray Baby Guerlain on her when she gets dressed in the morning and she loves it. She rubs it into her stomach and it is another little ritual we have together.'

The next day, my son and I braved the Guerlain perfume shop on the way home from our little ritual of making mud pies in the park. We were neither clean, nor fresh smelling. We inquired after Baby Guerlain at F200 a bottle. The nurse – or so she seemed in a pink dress and white shoes – sprayed a piece of cardboard for us each to sniff, and explained she also had a version with alcohol in it for the older child. My son crushed the cardboard tester in disgust and dropped it over the pram. As we tried to creep out of the shop without buying anything, the saleswoman came after us menacingly with an aerosol saying 'Would Madame like to be perfumed?' We ran for it.

I related this trauma to a British mother who lives in Paris. 'It is only a matter of time,' she predicted, 'before the French invent cellulite creams for those fat toddler thighs.'

Do not despair, however, if the Petit Bateau children's clothes chain leaves you bankrupt. After years of puzzlement, a French mother let me into the secret: Du Pareil Au Même, the children's clothes chain with branches across Paris, and childsize prices. Dungarees are Fr60, T shirts Fr30, coats Fr200, all in great colours in good cotton and wool, which last wash after wash. The stock changes every two weeks, there are rip-offs of designer labels, and if they made adult sizes, I'd never leave.

The 6th and 7th *arrondissements* are the best place for children's shopping. The basement of the Bon Marché department store, 38 Rue de Sèvres, 7th, M Sèvres-Babylone, 01 44 39 80 00, stocks almost every designer brand. The cheaper shops are down Rue St Placide, including: Du Pareil Au Même (and branches), 14 Rue St Placide, 6th, M Sèvres-Babylone, 01 45 44 04 40. Tout Compte Fait, 31 Rue St Placide, 6th, M Sèvres-Babylone, 01 42 22 45 64. The grander ones are around Boulevard St Germain including: Bonpoint, 67, Rue de l'Université, 7th, M Solférino, 01 45 55 63 70. Tartine et Chocolat, 266 Boulevard St Germain, 7th, M Solférino, 01 45 56 10 45. Jacadi, 256 Boulevard St Germain, 7th, M Solférino, 01 42 84 30 40.

"The magazine *L'Evénément du Jeudi* has pointed out that one of the most schizophrenic traits of the French is their ability to bang on about maintaining the *cuisine du terroir* while eating burgers by the million at Le McDo. Fortunately, Paris schools are fighting a rearguard action against junk food. There is now the Semaine de Goût (taste week), when Michelin-starred chefs go into schools in downtrodden neighbourhoods to advise children on creating a perfect *beurre blanc*.

I have also become a connoisseur of the menus posted outside schools for public reassurance. Our local state primary recently gave notice of the following luncheons for tiny gastronomes: Wednesday: *Carottes Rapées avec Oeuf Dur, Gigot d'Agneau, Jardinière des Legumes, Brie, Cerises. Gouter* [snack]: *Chausson de Pommes* (apple turnover). Thursday: *Salade de Lentilles et Tomates, Filet de Colin* [hake], *Pavé avec Citron, Choufleur au Gratin, Fromage Blanc, Fraises*.

A step above Britain's custard 'n' chips, and a clear attempt to follow the old Jesuit theory: 'Give me a set of tastebuds at the age of seven and they're mine for life.'

DISNEY-
LAND

Agent of pure wickedness

We did not go to Disney: Disney came to us. It began
imperceptibly, more than two years ago, when a French
person who should have been more patriotic brought my
eldest son a navy polo shirt embroidered with a tiny
Mickey. The Mouse was in our house.

Then the occasional McDonald's Happy Meal toy
slipped the exclusion zone: a plastic Pocohontas here, a
flapping Pegasus on wheels there. Inexplicably, my son
knew all the Disney characters' names, without ever seeing
a film. He identified Hercules on the only velcro-fastening
trainers that fitted him; he made erudite references to the
Lady and the Tramp spaghetti scene.

Disney merchandise entered our home as stealthily
as the fleas on the rats that brought the Black Death. Soon
the mouse held us in vice-like white gloves. My son was
infected and incurable. Without movie exposure, he
became Pongo the Dalmatian.

He also stood sadly in newsagents looking at *Lion
King* comics, and persistently pointed out Disneyland
advertisements in the *Figaro* magazine: 'The country with
the best cheese also has the best mouse,' they allege. By
pop-cultural osmosis, our three-year-old had learnt a) that

Disneyland existed and b) it was somewhere near Paris. His campaign began.

As the ads say: 'The magic is closer than you think'. Imagine our horror when we discover the Magic Kingdom is only 35 minutes from the Rue du Bac. We surrender to the powerful, irrevocable conclusion, and head down the A4 in the family Ford. 'That sign says Disneyland!' rejoices our son, who cannot read yet but can somehow recognize the shape of the Disney and Coco-Cola logos, name-branded on his brain from birth.

Intellectually, we are not unprepared. The day before, I'd gone to the American bookshop to buy *Team Rodent: How Disney devours the world*, an essay by the unrivalled ironist and novelist Carl Hiaasen. We have readings in the car. 'Disney is so good at being good that it manifests an evil; so uniformly efficient and courteous, so dependably clean and conscientious, so unfailingly *entertaining* that it's unreal and therefore is an agent of pure wickedness,' says Hiaasen. He reveals that Disney's imagineers are also profiteers, to the tune of $20 billion last year. Disney has 550 shops round the world. We're in a Mouse trap.

'Will we see Mickey and Minnie?' asks my son, interrupting from the back.

'If there's anything more irresistible than Jesus, it's Mickey,' says Hiaasen.

The Disneyland entry sign straddles six lanes of motorway. Sleeping Beauty's pink castle shimmers in the distance. There's a series of booths like an international border crossing, and it's hard to suppress the feeling you're entering a sovereign state with its own weird rules. You are. In America, the Magic Kingdom has its own blue-uniformed police force, and the sartorial codes here for staff smack of dictatorship: no make-up for women, no beards for men, no jewellery, no nail varnish.

But arriving outside the theme park, we realize that the downtrodden workers are in revolt, this particular week. The 'Zip-a-dee-doo-dah' Muzak is drowned out by drums, as disaffected employees wave banners complaining that Disney pays only the minimum wage. Mickey, Minnie, Goofy, Dumbo and over 200 other costumed characters are on strike, demanding to be respected and rewarded as 'artists', not mere furry friends.

The children look worried. Then we spot Captain Hook signing autographs. My son I gapes in amazement. All the swashbuckling makes him shy. 'Is it really Captain Hook?' he asks. 'Yes,' I answer. You can't tarnish a three-year-old's imagination with concepts like 'scab'.

Then we see Mickey Mouse. So do a hundred other people. There are so few furry characters around that the mob pursues him into a corner by the Disneyana Collectibles old-tyme store. People press cameras and snotty children into Mickey's face. He shifts uneasily from foot to foot, his smile a rictus. Kids are pulling his coat and poking him. Suddenly Mickey (probably an executive in disguise) freaks out, waves his white gloves in the air, and runs to safety behind a building.

Then we get down to the hard slog of queuing for rides – up to 45 minutes, but then it's a Saturday in July. What do we expect? No sensible family of four would pay nearly £60 for this. As it is, we adults barely make it through three hours before we hyperventilate and become tearful. It's too clean, too green, too perfect. As Hiaasen says; 'Disney is not in the business of exploiting nature so much as striving to improve upon it, constantly fine-tuning God's work.' We long for the smell of rancid chip fat and the death rattle of the Coney Island rollercoaster.

We escape Minnie and Winnie balloons, bobbing horribly in the car, blocking out all light. Returning to France and reality, we are comforted by a roadsign: Parc Astérix 46km.

1   DISNEYLAND PARIS, Marne-la-Vallée, RER A Marne-la-Vallée-
    Chessy, 01 64 74 30 00, Fr195 adult, Fr150 child.
2   PARC ASTÉRIX, Plailly, RER B to Roissy CDG + bus
    06 44 62 34 34, Fr160 adult, Fr110 child.

❝It appears that in Minnesota there are scholars who specialize in Disney studies. Professor Karel Ann Marling curated the Architecture of Reassurance: Designing the Disney Theme Parks exhibition and says that the 'masterstroke' of Disneyland was its 'hub and wienie' plan. The punter is first drawn to the central roundabout, or hub, which 'has untold psychological value, stressing the great American consumerist choice'. From there, he aims for a wienie or hot dog, an enormous phallic symbol in the sky, such as Sleeping Beauty's pink castle, or the rocket on Space Mountain. This wienie system provides 'a point of psychological assurance that signals you have arrived', according to Marling.

The Disney ethos seems oddly familiar to us Parisians: the 12 avenues radiating out from the hub of the Arc de Triomphe; the broad boulevards taking the eye to a focal point; the uniform façades of apartment blocks, none over a comforting six storeys; and the

national wienie, the Eiffel Tower. Baron Georges
Eugène Haussmann, architect of Paris, step forward
for your Mouseketeer award.